Modernist Estates —Europe

First published in 2019 by White Lion Publishing,
an imprint of The Quarto Group.
The Old Brewery, 6 Blundell Street,
London N7 9BH
United Kingdom
www.QuartoKnows.com

Modernist Estates Europe:
The buildings and the people who live in them today
Text © 2019 Stefi Orazi
Photography © 2019 Stefi Orazi unless otherwise credited
Design: Stefi Orazi Studio

Every effort has been made to trace the copyright holders
of material quoted in this book. If application is made in
writing to the publisher, any omissions will be included in
future editions.

A catalogue record for this book is available from
the British Library.
ISBN 978–0–7112–3908–1

Printed in China
10 9 8 7 6 5 4 3 2 1

Brimming with creative inspiration, how-to projects and useful
information to enrich your everyday life, Quarto Knows is a
favourite destination for those pursuing their interests and
passions. Visit our site and dig deeper with our books into your
area of interest: Quarto Creates, Quarto Cooks, Quarto Homes,
Quarto Lives, Quarto Drives, Quarto Explores, Quarto Gifts,
or Quarto Kids.

Modernist Estates —Europe

The buildings and the people who live in them today

by Stefi Orazi

WHITE LION

Cover
Section of the smaller house type at Siedlung Halen, Bern, Switzerland, designed by Atelier 5.

Acknowledgements
I would like to extend my special thanks to all the residents who generously contributed to the realisation of this book, to the staff at White Lion Publishing and to the following individuals: Emily Alston, Christine Bodin, Fabio Schmieder, Livia Lauber, Michael Evidon, Mia Nilsson and Harry Woodrow for their invaluable support, knowledge and contacts. To my sister Nicola Orazi for all her help, to Lucie Roberts and Damian Wayling for their generosity. A special thank you to LB for his continued guidance, and to Megi Zumstein and Claudio Barandun for their fine Swiss hospitality.

Contents

Introduction

Two weeks before the UK referendum on leaving the European Union, I made my first research trip for this book – to the Werkbund Estate in Vienna, built in the early 1930s by thirty-two European architects. My next destination would see me in Berlin, to Hansaviertel to explore its Interbau57 buildings by no fewer than fifty-three architects from Europe and beyond. While Britain spent the next two years wrangling on how to withdraw itself from the EU, I spent it feeling grateful that I could easily travel from one country to the next, reflecting on how that freedom also allowed many of the architects featured in this book to share ideas across country borders. So what lessons can we learn from mass housing across the continent, what similarities, what differences do they share, and after nearly ninety years since the building of the experimental Werkbund Estates, are they still places people can and want to live in today?

Choosing the estates I wanted to feature was an easy task. My bookshelves are filled with architecture books from the 1950s–70s of modern European housing, with black and white photography of crisp concrete or sharp brick buildings in cosmopolitan cities such as Berlin and Stockholm. I set across Europe wanting to explore some of the extraordinary estates and to find out if attitudes to modernist housing differs from country to country, meeting the residents who have chosen to live there and to see how these buildings have fared over the years.

The fifteen case studies in this book are of course only a snapshot and cannot by any means give a thorough picture or understanding of European housing. I was limited to featuring the estates where residents – strangers – kindly opened their doors to me, and regrettably was not able to get my foot inside anyone's home in Eastern Europe, whose buildings I have no doubt could easily fill the contents of a book on their own.

In the interwar years, new housing design in Europe was driven by the pursuit of improved sanitation, community, family life and healthy living, following years of poor living conditions that had caused epidemics such as tuberculosis. Early examples include the Bella Vista housing complex in Copenhagen by Arne Jacobsen and the Werkbund Estates in six cities across Europe. These favoured the 'garden city' approach of creating new communities on the outskirts of the city, typically white, sugar-cube-like houses with flat roofs that became synonymous with the Modern Movement.

This new building programme was short lived, however, as the Second World War broke out in 1939. The few countries that maintained neutrality during the war continued with their housing projects, albeit at a reduced rate, including Sweden, with influential schemes such as Backström and Reinius' point blocks in Danviksklippan. When the war ended, the rest of Europe followed suit with drive and ambition to rebuild the bomb-damaged towns and cities and to rehouse its citizens in decent homes. There was a sense of clearing away the past in order to create a new, fairer society and architects and governments embraced modernism as the answer to the housing crisis.

I was surprised to see just how many of the schemes I visited were influenced by Le Corbusier's renowned slab block the Unité d'habitation in Marseille. However, rather than create carbon copies, architects often took on the same qualities and disciplines of the Unité, but tried to improve on them to fit the local landscape or demographic. For example, in Atelier 5's Halen in Bern, the alternative to the vertical building was to opt for low-rise housing in mat planning form, to fit closely with the local topography. In the Bloco das Águas Livres building in Lisbon a more direct influence can be seen to the Unité, but here the architects made the proportions and materials of their building much grander for the middle classes that would inhabit it.

The majority of the schemes in this book are high quality 'prototypes' in collective housing – seminal examples – and many of them are protected and recognised for their architectural importance, but in order to build quickly and cheaply the preferred method of construction during the post-war years was system-building. In the UK, house building by the welfare state peaked in the 1960s – largely high-rise tower blocks – at just over 400,000 a year. France had a similar approach with its 'grand ensembles', large-scale housing estates on the outskirts of its cities, and Sweden had its 'Million Homes Programme'. This type of mass housing, which was initially met with approval and enthusiasm, was gradually displaced by doubts and criticised for creating inhumane and bland environments lacking communal facilities.

A number of architects in particular became critical of the welfare state in its creation of these mass-produced schemes and sought to offer an alternative, such as in Carlo Aymonino and Aldo Rossi's Monte Amiata project in Milan, and Jean Renaudie's Ivry-sur-Seine in Paris. The housing complex of Aymonino and Rossi looked to offer a complete new part of a city as a coherent urban element. It has over 100 variations of flat types across 440 units. In Ivry, Renaudie went even further, making no two units the same.

Of course such unique solutions in housing do not come cheap, and the question of who and how to fund homes is a pertinent one. The case studies in this book range from welfare state funded, such as Linksview House in Edinburgh, to privately funded schemes such as Halen outside Bern, with interesting models in between, including private/public collaborations. The Gallaratese II scheme, for example, was a financial investment by the Monte Amiata Mining company, who owned the land, but commissioned by the municipality of Milan. Aside from the Bloco das Águas Livres and Arne Jacobsen's work in Copenhagen, all of the schemes were initially conceived as being affordable, using industrialised materials and systems, and aimed at ordinary working families.

There is also the question of maintenance. These buildings are not cheap to maintain – many of them were built using new innovative materials and construction methods and are at a crucial point where they need extensive refurbishment and restoration. They were built in an era of cheap energy, when 'conservation' was not yet in the lexicon, with minimal insulation, single-glazed windows and ageing mechanical systems. Whether it be new windows, updating heating systems or treating concrete spalling, how do we best maintain these buildings, in a sympathetic way, preserving their architectural integrity while meeting modern standards, and who will foot the bill? As many of the buildings here are of exceptional historical importance, they are protected as architectural monuments and any work undertaken has to be approved. There is a fine line, however, between conservation and restoration, and ensuring people do not feel as if they are living in a museum.

I first visited the Werkbund Estate in Vienna in 1998, and despite it having been listed as an official national monument in 1978, the houses were in very poor condition. By my second visit in 2016 the whole estate had been transformed – restored with the same materials and techniques that were used during the original construction in 1932. However, the resident I visited, despite loving the architecture, felt too restricted. Not being able to paint the walls the colour of your choosing, or being able to install a modern fitted kitchen, surely goes against the very principles Josef Frank, the initiator and artistic director of the Vienna scheme, had set out.

Atelier 5's Halen, Bern is faced with a similar problem. I was lucky to have the opportunity to meet with two of the original architects, who still live on the estate today. Their concept for the housing was that it should be flexible. A house should have the ability to change and adapt just as a growing family does – no interior wall is structural, for example, allowing you to change the interior layout as you see fit. In fact, ninety-three-year-old Hans Hosteller, one of the founding architects, and his wife had done just this, converting what would have originally been the children's bedroom on the lower ground floor, which opens on to the garden, into their main living space. In 2003 the estate became listed as a Swiss Heritage Site, preventing any alterations, again going against the very principles of the architects' vision.

Of all the schemes I visited, the most successful were the ones where the housing offered the maximum amount of flexibility, privacy within their own homes but the opportunity for neighbourliness. As in Halen, or in Walden 7, Barcelona with its unique module system consisting of combinations of 30 square-metre units distributed over one or two floors, allowing dwellings to be formatted in single-module studios to four-module apartments and back again depending on the size of your family.

The success of the communal spaces across the schemes and typologies I visited was mixed. The impressive amphitheatre in Monte Amiata was empty on my visit. The internal 'shopping street' in Le Corbusier's Cité Radieuse, apart from a bakery, could hardly be deemed as a useful group of shops; however, the fantastic roof terrace was being occupied by an energetic Zumba class. The children's parks outside the Tanto blocks in Stockholm were full with children and their parents nattering on the sidelines. It seemed to me the schemes that were designed with the nuclear family in mind worked best when they were still inhabited by young families. In Halen, where communal space such as the swimming pools are jointly owned by the residents, the sense of community seemed very strong, with tales of front doors being left open and children running in and out of each other's homes – not dissimilar to the stories told by the original residents of the Danielle Casanova building in Ivry-sur-Seine, Paris and Walden 7, Barcelona in the 1960s and 70s.

The role of the architect in society following the post-war building programmes has been greatly reduced in recent times. Today an architect may only be brought in at the planning stage, which is a far cry from their heyday when they were at the forefront of innovation, tasked with the role of devising new ways of living. The role of the welfare state as the main provider of the social necessities such as housing is also diminishing, leaving it instead to the market and the private sector to provide. It is no coincidence that Vienna has the most extensive social housing programme in Europe and regularly tops the Mercer 'Quality of Living' survey. More than 80 per cent of residents rent, and two-thirds live in subsidised housing.

It is also interesting to note that many of the buildings in this book that were conceived as being affordable to rent, are now privately owned. Housing in the public sector in Europe in recent decades is being sold to tenants or private companies in order to generate revenue. The apartment blocks in Hansarviertel in Berlin are now nearly all privately owned, as too are the Tanto apartments in Stockholm, and of course throughout Britain due to the Thatcher government-initiated Right-to-Buy scheme. To my mind the egalitarian spirit of modernist collective housing across Europe, with its ambition of making good-quality, well-designed homes available to ordinary people and its thriving communities, will be lost if we continue the selling off or demolishing of our post-war housing. We will be faced with growing inequality and a housing shortage all over again, the very problem these schemes and their architects aimed to solve.

10

Bellevue

Copenhagen Denmark

Architect Arne Jacobsen

In the 1930s, a period when living conditions for many people were often cramped, lacked sunlight and decent sanitation, came the recognition of the beneficial qualities of the sun and sea to one's mental and physical health. Between the years of 1931 and 1951 Danish architect Arne Jacobsen (1902–71) was responsible for a number of projects in Klampenborg, a northern suburb of Copenhagen. His work began there after winning a competition run by Gentofte Municipality for the design of a seaside resort complex of Bellevue beach. Jacobsen designed every element of the resort from changing booths, blue-striped lifeguard towers and ice cream parlours to the ice cream packaging itself. In June 1932 Bellevue beach was inaugurated by the Danish Prime Minister and it soon became the most popular resort in Copenhagen.

Further commissions by the municipality followed, including the Bellavista housing complex, completed in 1934. The site had been home to a country house which was demolished to make way for sixty-eight new apartments. Bellavista follows the style of the International Modern Movement, partly due to the council setting various restrictions for the new buildings. Principally they were to be no more than three storeys, and only two storeys along the main road, Strandvejen, with a preference for white facades and flat roofs. The buildings are arranged in a staggered U-shape, with apartments oriented towards the sun, each with a generous private balcony that looks over the Øresund. The apartments were well equipped with modern amenities such as central heating, garages and rubbish shoots, clearly aimed at an affluent market.

Further projects for Jacobsen followed, including the Texaco petrol station with its unique mushroom-like canopy, the Mattson's Riding School and the Bellevue Theatre and Restaurant. The theatre building is positioned perpendicular to Strandvejen, and the restaurant is attached to it but faces away from the road in a sweeping manner, to give its customers the best possible views. A relationship between these buildings and the Bellavista complex is created with the use of similar materials, the height and white facades. The restaurant was just over 60 metres long and nearly 10 metres wide, and could be divided in two by a sliding partition. There was also a dining terrace and private dining rooms. The theatre and restaurant were completed in 1937, but due to its size the restaurant was hard to fill and shut down in 1950. It was converted to housing by architect Niels Rohweder in 1951, but the exterior remains largely unchanged.

Arne Jacobsen spent two years in exile in Stockholm during the Second World War but returned to Copenhagen in 1945 when he was commissioned to design the Søholm terrace housing, 400 metres south of Bellavista. The row housing marked a departure in style from the Bellavista apartments, reflecting the post-war trend for more traditional brick construction. The development, completed in three stages, consists of chained and terraced houses comprising a total of eighteen units. For each stage, Jacobsen designed houses of different types: Søholm I to the south has five houses, Søholm II to the west nine houses and Søholm III to the north has four houses. The result is simple, clean and unostentatious homes. In 1951, Jacobsen decided to build his own house, studio and garden in Søholm, and he lived there until his death in 1971.

Opposite
Bellavista housing taken in the 1930s

Pages 12–13
The former Bellevue Theatre Restaurant, converted into apartments in the 1950s

Pages 14–15
Søholm terrace housing (left) and the Bellavista apartments (right)

Mads Hage Thomsen and Lone Juul

Mads, a television studio designer, and Lone, who works in the film and television industry, have two children. They live in what used to be the Bellevue Theatre Restaurant. In 1951 the restaurant was converted into apartments.

How did you come to live in Bellevue?
[M] We've been living here together since 1994, but I actually grew up here in the 1970s. My family owned a couple of these apartments back then. When I moved back here with Lone we initially lived in a smaller flat in the middle of the building that used to belong to my father. Then once our children were born, we moved to this larger one which my uncle used to own.

Lone, what was your first impression when you came here?
[L] I knew about the buildings already because of the famous Bellevue Theatre next door, and I would come to the beach with friends when I was young. When I went inside our first apartment, though, I really wanted to live here, I really liked it.

What was it like growing up as a child here, Mads?
[M] It was a bit boring to be honest, there's not much happening out here. There were a lot of old people, and there are no shops. But you have nature, the beach and it's close to Copenhagen.

So these apartments were originally a restaurant; can you tell me a bit more about that?
[M] It was built as a restaurant in the 1930s, so the building was one long room with a very high ceiling. Because of the size, it was very hard to fill and to get people to come out here, and by the 1950s it had closed down. It was then converted into apartments by the Danish architect Niels Rohweder in 1951 – the exterior is mainly unchanged and as Arne Jacobsen designed it.

Does a converted restaurant work as a family home?
[L] Yes, I think so. It's not a traditional family house where the children can just go out and play in the street, but it works for us.

Are there many other families living here?
[M] There are a few – my best friend lives next door, and he has children. Generally, people don't tend to move out of here. In this apartment, for example, we are only the third people to live here. So it tends to be when the old people die, younger families then move in.

Have you done much to the apartment since you moved in?
[L] A little, the kitchen was originally downstairs – a small room but with a 5-metre-high ceiling – so we moved it upstairs and added a bedroom up there also.

You mentioned earlier, Mads, that when you were growing up here there were a lot of older people living in the area. Has that changed?
[M] I think there are still a lot of old people living here.
[L] But in the Bellavista apartments, I have noticed some younger families recently. When we first moved here I remember seeing a lot of old people from Bellavista walking down to the beach first thing in the morning to go 'winter bathing', and they would take almost an hour to walk down there! Now there are not as many.

You mentioned there isn't a lot to do around here…
[L] There isn't so much in the way of shops or restaurants in the immediate area, but we are so close to Copenhagen so if you want to go out for a drink it's only twelve minutes on the train. But we have the beach and nature, which is great for us as we have a dog, so we go walking. When my daughter lived here she used to go horse-riding at the riding school next door, also designed by Jacobsen, and of course we have the theatre too.

The area must feel very different in the summer?
[L] Yes, if it's sunny and warm there are people everywhere. There's a continuous stream of people coming off the train that seems never ending. That lasts for two months or so.
[M] But even out of season, if it's a sunny day then it is still a popular destination. The road between us and the beach runs all the way along the coast, and it's a beautiful drive, so people stop off here at the beach and have an ice cream or whatever.

Do you get a lot of people coming to visit the area to look at the architecture?
[M] Yes, it is very well known. We get a lot of architects coming out here taking pictures. People don't often realise that these apartments are here, or they get confused and think it's part of Bellavista.

Do people move here because of the architecture?
[L] When people first move here all they talk about is keeping things 'original', but the inside isn't original Jacobsen anyway. For us it's just our home and we don't think about it as we've lived here for so long.

Is the inside of the building listed?
[M] Yes, we need to get permission to do any work. We are currently redoing the facade of the building and that's a big project which I am quite involved in. The Bellavista apartments recently renovated the outside of their buildings, but they didn't do it in the original way so it's a lot whiter than it would have been. We want to do it right, in lime plaster and chalk.

Who makes those kind of decisions, that affect the whole building?
[M] There are sixteen of us that live here, so we all get together as an association and discuss and make decisions.
[L] Mads has spent a long time working on the facade, finding the right contractors and so on, but he enjoys it as he wants to make sure it's done properly.

Are there any other implications to living in such a building? You have so much glazing, for example, and high ceilings – is it difficult to heat the place?
[M] Originally the windows were sash and they were very draughty. It was an experimental way of building so the window frames were very thin – beautiful but not so practical. Living so close to the sea it can get really windy, you wouldn't even have been able to have a candle lit. We were allowed to change them and they are a lot better now; in fact, we are going to replace them again in the next couple of years and that will make a big difference to the insulation.

What's the best thing about living here?
[M] I love sitting in the dining room and looking out towards the sea. I like the fact you are outside of the city but easily connected to it.
[L] I agree. We once thought about moving when the children were little, but you can't beat the view — every day you look out and it's different.

Opposite
The main living space

Above left
The hallway looking towards the children's bedrooms

Above right
The living space with views towards the Øresund

Above
Stairs leading up to the mezzanine level

Above left
The kitchen on the first floor

Above right
The dining area on the mezzanine level

Werkbundsiedlung Neubühl

Zurich Switzerland

Architects Paul Artaria, Max Ernst Haefeli, Carl Hubacher, Werner Max Moser, Emil Roth, Hans Schmidt and Rudolf Steiger

Following the First World War, the Deutscher Werkbund – a German association of artists, designers, industrialists and architects – commissioned leading European architects including Mies van der Rohe, Walter Gropius and Le Corbusier to showcase a new model for domestic housing. This took the form of a living exhibition in Stuttgart in 1927 – the Weissenhof Estate comprising sixty dwellings. The exhibition allowed visitors to personally experience a new vision of society through architecture in the International Style, based around the ideals of reducing costs, simplifying housekeeping and improving living conditions.

A number of similar exhibitions followed in Brno, Breslau, Prague, Vienna (see page 39) and Zurich – unified by their architectural appearance of simplified facades and flat roofs, and an aspiration to tackle the housing shortage through new building techniques, materials and technology. The Werkbundsiedlung Neubühl was the largest of all the developments, and unlike other projects which were subsided by the state, Neubühl was completely self-funded and had to compete on the open market.

The project was conceived by a group of young architects: Max Ernst Haefeli (1901–76), Carl Hubacher (1897–1990), Rudolf Steiger (1900–82), Werner Max Moser (1896–1970), Emil Roth (1893–1980), Paul Artaria (1892–1959), Hans Schmidt (1893–1972) and the general secretary of the Swiss Werkbund Friedrich T. Gubler (1900–65), as a non-profit housing co-operative. Assisted by their parents, the architects acquired an attractive plot of land in Wollishofen, a southern district of Zurich. The group, who worked collaboratively from planning to conception, strived to preserve the views of Lake Zurich and the valley from the houses, and proposed two new streets parallel to an existing street. The municipality agreed on the basis that the project would be completed in three phases.

The houses are arranged in simple rows perpendicular to the streets, making the most of the sun and light as well as creating better noise insulation. Great emphasis was placed on the landscaping, which was designed by the well-known Swiss landscape architect Gustav Ammann. He was inspired by the natural landscaping of English gardens, and existing trees were preserved as much as possible. The houses each have large picture windows overlooking generous private gardens, forming a direct connection between the inside and outside.

Completed in 1932, the final scheme comprises 195 units in a wide variety of types: 105 houses ranging from two-storey to three-storey, and 90 apartments ranging from one-room to six-room units. There were also thirty-two one-car garages, four retail units, a primary school and apartments that could be rented out to friends and family.

A number of restorations have taken place over the years. In 1986 there was a complete renovation and each house was restored to its original condition. More recently, facades, roofs, windows and doors have been upgraded to the original designs and in 2010 the estate was listed, protecting it both internally and externally. Today the estate is immaculately preserved, with a number of 'museum houses' – dwellings that are inhabited but are open to the public at certain times.

Opposite
Birds-eye view of Neubühl, taken shortly after completion

Pages 24–27
Houses at Neubühl with paths that run perpendicular to the main roads

Werkbundsiedlung Neubühl,
Zurich, Switzerland

Architects: Paul Artaria, Max Ernst Haefeli, Carl Hubacher,
Werner Max Moser, Emil Roth, Hans Schmidt and Rudolf Steiger

Miriam Lendenmann and Victor Pérez de Arce

Miriam, currently a student, and her husband Victor, a chef originally from Chile, live in a four-bedroom house with their two children.

How long have you lived in Siedlung Neubühl for?
[M] We have been in this house since April, but we used to live close by in an apartment. We had our eye on this particular house – every time we went by it I thought, 'that would be my dream house'. The previous tenant, a lady who lived here for over sixty years, passed away and, somehow, we managed to get the house. When I became pregnant with my first child, we were living in the centre of Zurich, in what is sort of the red light district. We put our names on the list for Siedlung Neubühl, but never imagined getting a place here so quickly.

Are the houses sought after?
Yes, there is a long waiting list of people wanting to get houses. We were lucky because we knew someone here, and that helped.

What was it about Siedlung Neubühl that made you want to live here?
I grew up nearby, on the other side of the hill, and had friends who lived in Neubühl. They seemed to have a great childhood growing up here, so it was one of my goals to bring up my children here.

Has it changed much since you were a child?
Not at all. Around thirty years ago it became a protected area, so you can't alter the structure of the buildings. Before that some people made changes, such as knocking down walls between the kitchen and living room, but you couldn't do that now. Generally, the architecture and the way the houses look has always been appreciated by its residents.

Are the houses rented or owned?
They are all rented, you can't buy them. It is run as a co-operative, so the rent is really low and kept that way. It's very affordable, and the cheapest you can find for a house in Zurich. Originally, they were meant for people on low incomes, but now anyone is allowed to rent them.

What is the community like?
It used to be mainly old people because it was part of the lease agreement that once you were here, you could stay forever. But in the last few years more families have moved in and more children have been born. Recently, the lease changed – you now have to move out five years after your children grow up and leave home. There are a lot of opportunities to get to know your neighbours if you want to. For example, there are regular events organised by the residents, especially for the children, such as barbecues and so on. But if you prefer not to socialise and be involved, that's also okay.

What's the area like?
This area is classed as part of the city centre, but we are about 6 kilometres away. If you depend on public transport, then that's not so great. People in Zurich expect a bus every five minutes, but here you have to wait fifteen minutes. That can make it feel a bit disconnected, but it's not a problem for us as it's only a twenty-minute cycle to the centre. I think there are positives and negatives. I love the fact that you can walk five minutes and be in a farm with cows, but twenty minutes in another direction and you can be in the centre, with all the shops, restaurants etc.

What's the best thing about living here?
The fact that the children can play freely in a 'safe bubble'. It's really green – they can climb trees, run around and play with the other children here.

And the worst?
I really can't think of anything that bothers me about living here.

Are all the houses the same size?
The houses vary. Ours, and the others in this row, are all five-room, but in the next row they are six-room houses. However, to be eligible for the bigger ones you need to have at least three children. All the houses have private gardens, and there are communal gardens with vegetable patches for everyone to share. There is also a block of apartments which vary a lot in size, and don't have gardens.

What is it specifically about the house that you like?
The living room is really spacious, as it's actually the living and dining room in one. The full-width windows let in a lot of light, which is really unusual in an old house. It feels modern but old at the same time, which I like. The architects had great ideas – for example, we can completely open up the windows in the living room and 'bring in the garden'.

Does the house feel big enough for the four of you?
Yes, even though the rooms upstairs are small – we just don't clutter them up too much with furniture. That's also something that the architects intended – for the rooms to have a lot of air circulating through them.

The house is coming close to being 100 years old – does it still work in the twenty-first century for a modern family?
Yes, it does, the way it was designed feels timeless. I wouldn't feel comfortable in a new building, but old buildings are also problematic. The house has been almost completely renewed in terms of wiring, plumbing, windows etc. so it functions well. There are some houses where the kitchens are still original, and those can't be changed and are kept as 'museum houses'. As I am a student and Victor is a chef, we don't earn that much money, so we never thought we would be able to get out of living in an apartment. We feel really blessed that we can live in such a house with a garden.

Above
The open plan living and dining room with full-width glazing, looking on to the back garden

Opposite
The kitchen with views towards the mountains

Right
The living room with access to the back garden

Above
Kitchen hatch looking into the living space

Above
Upstairs landing, looking towards the bathroom,
with the bedrooms on the left and right

35

Above left
The main bedroom

Above right
Built-in wardrobe in the main bedroom

Above left and right
The two children's bedrooms

Werkbund-siedlung

Vienna Austria

32 Architects including Josef Frank, Adolf Loos, Richard Neutra, Margarete Schütte-Lihotzky and Gerrit Rietveld

The period between 1919 and 1934, known as 'Red Vienna', saw the city facing an acute decent housing shortage. Following the First World War, the Social Democrats' administration of Vienna sought to tackle the crisis by instigating a mass building programme, which took the form of multi-storey municipal apartment buildings. In a ten-year period over 64,000 dwellings were built. Aimed at the working classes, the apartments were generally between 38 and 48 square metres and offered basic amenities such as running water, windows in each room and communal facilities, including bath houses, laundry rooms and kindergartens.

The Vienna Werkbund houses, located in the 13th district of Heitzing, looked to offer an alternative model to the affordable housing of the 'Red Vienna' municipal blocks, with individual family units with gardens. The Austrian Werkbund, based on the model of the German Werkbund of artists, architects, entrepreneurs and craftspeople, was founded in 1912 and its members included Josef Frank (1885–1967), Josef Hoffmann (1870–1956) and Oskar Strnad (1879–1935). Frank became a central figure and the initiator of the Vienna Werkbund estate.

The estate shared many of the principals of other Werkbund housing schemes, aiming to showcase the latest developments in modern housing and interior design. It was, however, less concerned with the unified aesthetic of the International Style and focused instead on offering individuality and serving the needs of the occupants. This can be seen in the facades of the houses where the colour scheme, developed by the artist László Gábor, emphasises the differences between the buildings. Although some were painted white, the majority are in pastel shades of yellow, green and pink.

The exhibition to open the houses to the public had been planned for 1930, but changes to the way the houses were to be designed delayed the project by two years. The original scheme included both individual family houses and some apartment blocks, and was intended as affordable housing for rent in a working-class district of Vienna. A change in the location to a semi-rural area, however, called for a complete redesign and the houses were marketed for private ownership to the upper-middle classes instead.

Thirty-two architects were involved in the project; unlike the Zurich Werkbund, each architect came up with a different design solution based on roughly the same footprint, making the most efficient use of space in their own way. The urban planning of the houses was undertaken by Frank, who designed gently curving, natural looking paths that lead from the existing road into the centre of the estate, where he placed a small open space. Seventy-six houses were built and the exhibition opened in 1932. The houses were shown fully furnished with furniture designed by the architects. Frank believed, however, that the interiors should be flexible and occupants should have the freedom of choice when it came to the interior design.

More than 10,000 people visited the exhibition and it garnered wide international press coverage. However, Austria, as with much of the world in the early 1930s, was still in a depression, which meant that most people could not afford the high cost of the new houses. Fourteen were sold before the exhibition, but none afterwards. In 1938 the municipality of Vienna took ownership of fifty-six houses for social rent. Six of the houses were destroyed in the Second World War and the following years saw a decline in the maintenance of the remaining houses. Considered one of the most important examples of modern architecture in Vienna, in 2011 the Austrian Federal Monuments office on the initiative of Wohnbaus, a team of restorers and technicians, began a renovation programme. At a cost of 10 million euros, many of the houses are now fully restored and sensitively modernised.

Opposite
The Werkbundsiedlung on its opening day, 4 June 1932

Page 40
Houses designed by Gerrit Rietveld

Page 41
Houses designed by André Lurçat

Werkbundsiedlung, Vienna, Austria

Architects: Thirty-two, including Josef Frank, Adolf Loos, Richard Neutra, Margarete Schütte-Lihotzky and Gerrit Rietveld

Barbara Göttlinger

Barbara manages a French cosmetics shop in the local area as well as being a part-time ceramicist. She lives in a house designed by Gerrit Rietveld.

How long have you lived here?
The house was completely renovated, inside and out, about five years ago. I moved in shortly after it was completed. More than one hundred people applied to rent the house, so it wasn't easy to get it, but I applied along with my daughter, and I think they gave it to us because we were two women and they thought we would look after it.

Why did you want to live in this house?
I particularly liked the light as there are so many windows. I also liked the style of the house and the architecture.

Describe the layout of the house
The house is arranged over three floors plus a basement. On the ground floor, to the left of the entrance, is the kitchen and straight on is the living room – which I think is the best room in the house as it has fantastic light and access to the garden. On the first floor are two bedrooms and a small bathroom, and on the top floor is a small room, that I use as a library and my bedroom.

The house also has a lot of outside space, doesn't it?
Yes, two of the bedrooms have a terrace which run the full width of the house, but I don't use them. There are so many stairs in the house, which I found interesting when I first moved here, but now after five years of running up and down the narrow stairs every time you want something from the kitchen, it's becoming a problem.

Were all the houses on the estate renovated?
All the exteriors of the houses were, but they only renovated the interiors of the ten houses that were empty. My house was very dilapidated before the work, and they restored it to how it would have been when Rietveld designed it. They restored all the old linoleum floors, for example, and painted all the doors the original colour. The initial idea was that this house would be used as a museum, but the municipality of Vienna changed their mind and decided to let it out instead. In my opinion, it wasn't a good renovation as it's not comfortable to live here. The windows are all original and are draughty, the walls are thin and weren't insulated so it's very difficult and expensive to heat.

So does it feel like you are living in a museum?
Yes, sometimes. We can't make any changes to the house at all. I'm used to living in a very different style of house and I wanted to knock down some walls and open it up, but that's not allowed. We can't even change the colour of the walls or the doors. We have to be really careful to look after everything, such as the original floors which can't get too wet as it might ruin them. At first this was okay, but now I would like to live somewhere where I can do what I want to it.

Do you feel like you are part of a community, somewhere special?
Not really, we have a mixture of people living here which doesn't always work. The houses that have been renovated are very expensive to rent, but the other houses are for people with low incomes, so the rent is very low. That causes a bit of conflict. I don't think the houses work well for families and children. There are a lot of old people that have lived here for a very long time and I don't think having this mix of people works.

What's the best thing about living here?
My garden and the location.

What is the local area like?
We are in the 13th district which is a very wealthy area and very desirable in Vienna. You have everything here – good shops, schools and you are not too far from the centre. There are a lot of parks and the famous Baroque Schönbrunn Palace.

Do you think a house that was designed over eighty-five years ago can work in the twenty-first century?
I think if it is a properly thought-through renovation, then yes. The interiors need to be modernised – adding insulation, for example – so that you can live in them today. We shouldn't treat homes as if they are museums.

Opposite
The hallway, looking towards the living room

Above left
View of the staircase on the ground floor

Above right
View of the kitchen from the hallway

Above
The dining/living room

Opposite
The living space, with windows looking
over the garden

Above left
First floor landing space

Above right
One of four bedrooms

Opposite
View from the bedroom on the first floor
looking towards the bathroom. Stairs
leading up to the second floor, where
there are two further bedrooms

Danviksklippan

Stockholm Sweden

Architects Sven Backström and Leif Reinius

Mass housing in the mid-twentieth century in Europe tended to fall into one of two camps: it either followed the Le Corbusier slab block model, or the point block model. Derivatives of Le Corbusier's Unité d'habitation in Marseille were built across Europe during the post-war period, with varying levels of quality and success. Whereas the Unité was placed in isolation in the middle of a park, most other schemes could not afford the luxury of space, and large parallel blocks were often placed only 30–50 metres apart. Such schemes came under criticism and in a number of countries, especially in the UK (as seen in Harlow New Town), point blocks became the favoured model as they were deemed more 'human in scale'. This type of building is essentially a free-standing high-rise tower, with a central core for lifts and units all around – usually four per floor. The clear advantage is that each side of the building benefits from sunlight, meaning apartments could have windows on two sides.

There are many examples of point blocks in Sweden, where they originated. One of the earliest examples is at Danviksklippan on the edge of Stockholm, designed between 1943 and 1945 by Swedish architects Sven Backström (1903–92) and Leif Reinius (1907–95). At the time the development was widely regarded as among the best of its kind. The scheme comprises nine buildings in a group placed on the rocky Danvik cliff. The towers can be seen from afar, rising like monolithic blocks.

There are two types of buildings in the scheme, one with six apartments per floor and the other with eight per floor, with a total of approximately 400 apartments. Staircases, bathrooms and toilets are placed towards the centre of the building where there is no natural light, while the other rooms are placed to benefit from plenty of natural light. All apartments have private south-facing balconies. The corners of the towers are splayed and have a characteristic pointed pitched roof – they are fondly known as 'the pencil buildings'. The towers vary in height, with the tallest placed at the top of the cliff, and are spaced roughly twice their own width apart. In the middle of the scheme is a communal park designed by Walter Bauer. Another advantage of the point block over the slab block model, is that it offers minimum interference with the open space; buildings can be placed in a way that follows the contours of the ground formation.

Although the point block in Sweden was very successful, the high-quality build of Danviksklippan was not implemented across the country on a mass scale in the post-war period. Throughout the twentieth century during its housing shortage, Sweden had a commitment to raise the standard of living for all its citizens. The government ensured housing was kept out of the hands of financial speculators and instead favoured tenant-owned co-operatives, municipal-owned building companies and rent-controlled apartments. A policy after the Second World War, introduced by the Swedish Democratic Party, led to a democratisation of housing in terms of equality and inclusiveness. The 'Million Homes Programme' introduced in 1964 committed to build a million dwellings in the space of ten years. A third of those were single family dwellings, one-third were blocks of three storeys or less and the last third were high-rises with four storeys or more. To achieve this ambitious level of building, industrialised and pre-fabricated systems were used. The programme was barely halfway through when the housing shortage became a housing surplus, and criticisms were voiced about what some people perceived as uniform, and poor, architecture.

Opposite
The newly built point blocks on the Danvik cliff, 1944

Pages 52–53
The buildings today, facing the Danvik canal

Fredrik Jansson

Artist Fredrik lives with his partner in a one-bedroom apartment on the sixth floor. They have recently had their first child.

How long ago did you move here?
About seven years ago, but I've known about this place all of my life as I grew up nearby. I always liked the idea of a small community living on top of a rock.

Are the buildings well known?
They are to people who have lived in the area a long time, and also to commuters. We are right next to the motorway, so people from the suburbs heading into the city pass us every day. They refer to the buildings as the 'pencils' or 'rockets' because of their shape. Although a lot of people pass by in cars, it's not really a place you come to or end up in because it's up on a cliff.

What sort of community is there here?
It's a very quiet area and a lot of older people live here that have been here since the start.

So there aren't many other young families like yourself?
Not very many. We have a little playground here, but it's not used very much. Initially there would have been a lot more families, I think, in the 1940s and 50s; it generally used to be a lot busier. There used to be a fountain in the centre, for example, and also a couple of shops at the bottom of every building.

When did they shut?
I'm not sure. I guess everybody started to do their shopping in the city, so they went out of business. In the beginning it was the kind of place where you didn't need to leave. Everything was here on your doorstep – a butcher, greengrocers, a place to repair your shoes. Now that's all gone; all we have is a little corner shop and a pizza place.

What was it about Danviksklippan that you liked that made you want to live here?
I like the location – it's so close to the city, but yet we are not in it, we are just on the border. I like that it's so close to nature – the forest is just across the way and the archipelagos start here. Many of my friends, as well as my parents, live close by in the neighbouring suburbs.

Do you rent or own your home?
We bought it, but I think there are more rental properties here than owned. Anyone who rents has the opportunity to buy their apartment; that's been a big thing here in Stockholm over the last ten years or so.

Is it difficult to find a place to live here?
I've noticed prices going up recently. Everyone really loves the Danvik cliff, and I think people are beginning to notice this area.

Who manages the buildings?
Each block has its own board and is in charge of its own management. The small things in our own apartments we sort out ourselves, but for bigger things we would hire a firm to do those for us. For example, a few months ago, we had all the balconies replaced as they were falling apart. As we had to get them replaced like-for-like it was quite a big job and lasted about five months.

Are there any other signs of the building showing its age?
It all needs repairing all the time! When they came to replace the balconies they took the old ones down with a jack hammer and everything was shaking – the ceiling plaster all came down. I think when you are repairing old buildings like this you really need to do your homework and be sensitive to how it's built – not enter it with a jack hammer!

What's it like having a baby here; does it feel big enough for a family in the twentieth century?
Yes, we don't feel we need much space. The only thing is the walls are very thin. Our neighbours also have a baby, so if theirs wakes up and starts screaming, then so does ours – and vice versa!

Above left
The hallway

Above right
Looking towards the dining area from the living room

Opposite
The kitchen, with the dining room beyond

Opposite
The living room with views towards the
other point blocks of Danviksklippan

Above left
The bedroom

Above right
Communal entrance lobby to the building

Cité Radieuse

Marseille France

Architect Le Corbusier

It is hard to think of an architect who has influenced the landscape of modern housing in Europe more than Le Corbusier, and in particular his Unité d'habitation building in Marseille in the South of France. Born Charles-Édouard Jeanneret (1887–1965) in north-west Switzerland (he did not change his name to Le Corbusier until 1920), he spent much of his early adulthood exploring and travelling Europe, before he finally settled in Paris in 1917.

Housing in Europe in the 1920s generally followed either the 'block system', as in Vienna or Rotterdam, or a 'strip development' based on units of four or five storeys high, as in Berlin or Frankfurt. At the International Congresses of Modern Architecture (CIAM) in 1930, a high-rise slab-shaped apartment building was proposed as a standard solution to the European housing crisis. France, however, did not partake in any large-scale projects in this direction until after the Second World War. In the thirty years following Le Corbusier's Immeubles Villas project of 1922, he designed over thirty housing developments, but only a few were realised before his Marseille commission by the French Minister of Housing Raoul Dautry. The devastation caused by the war gave Le Corbusier the opportunity to realise his Unité d'habitation a grandeur conform (dwelling units of congruent size) in 1945.

The design of the scheme faced considerable opposition. With claims by health experts that the building would produce mental illness among its occupants, it was nicknamed 'Maison du Fada' (the madhouse). The Ministers of Reconstruction, however, thought of the project as a prototype for France's reconstruction, and were determined for it to go ahead. The building was completed in 1952.

Situated in one of Marseille's most beautiful districts, the seventeen-storey slab named 'La Cité Radieuse' (Radiant City) is raised off the ground on piloti on a huge reinforced concrete frame, with 337 structurally independent units inserted into the grid-like frame. Le Corbusier had been influenced by his visit to the Carthusian monastery of Ema, near Florence, in 1907 and the notion of individual units then arranged and collected together. He developed his grid using a proportional measurement system based on his 'Modulor Man' of 1943 – a concept that combined the proportions of a six-foot tall human figure with the mathematics of the golden ratio.

The Unité is 165 metres long and 56 metres high, set in the heart of a large park. Housing 1,600 people, a typical unit is dual aspect, split-level with a two-storey living room. To the east there are views of mountains and to the west, views of the sea. The units are served by 'internal streets' on every third floor, with two floors of shopping facilities halfway up the building. There are a number of communal facilities including a hotel, a kindergarten, a roof terrace with a gymnasium, a running track, an open-air theatre and a small swimming pool, all incorporated to promote a healthy life under open skies, free from traffic and in contact with nature.

To encourage a mixed community there are a total of twenty-three variations and sizes of apartments. Internally, they were fitted with simple mass-produced furniture and built-in storage designed by Jean Prouvé and Charlotte Perriand. Externally, the exposed concrete structure (béton brut) displays rough textures and the imperfections of the wood plank moulds used to make it.

The Cité Radieuse was the first building in which the 'modulor' system of proportions was used by Le Corbusier. He would go on to design several variations of the Unité in Nantes-Rezé, Briey en Forêt, Berlin, Meaux (unbuilt) and Firminy. Marseille, however, is the only one where the architect's complete vision was realised.

Opposite
La Cité Radieuse, circa 1952

Page 62
View towards the entrance of the building

Page 63
One of the 'internal streets'

Pages 64–65
The rooftop

Artemis Kosta and Laurent Perrinet

Artemis, originally from Greece, is a researcher in biology and her partner Laurent, a native of France, is a researcher in neuroscience. They live on the first floor with their two young sons.

Describe your apartment
[A] There are many different types of apartment layouts in the building, from small studios to much bigger family units. Ours is the most typical configuration. The apartments interlock, so with our neighbours' flat you go in and up the stairs, whereas we go in, and down. When you enter our apartment there is a small kitchen on the left and the dining room ahead – that overlooks the double height space below of the living room, which is also our bedroom.

The lower floor is double aspect, with our room facing west and the children's room facing east – both have a balcony. Our configuration is mainly original, but a lot of the apartments have closed off the double height space to create another room, which then also closes off the main bedroom downstairs and makes it more private. There were originally two children's bedrooms, separated by a sliding door, but that had been removed when we moved in, and our children prefer to share a room anyway.

What attracted you to moving here?
Laurent bought it just before we met. He's French and I'm originally from Greece. He grew up in a purpose-built apartment in Bordeaux so I think he liked the style of architecture. He was also working near here, and these apartments are around the same price as any others in the area, despite being designed by Le Corbusier.

What did you think of it the first time you saw it?
I liked it a lot. When Laurent first moved in he didn't have much stuff, so it felt very spacious. I was impressed! It was only after we had the children that we started to accumulate things, and now I think maybe when the boys are teenagers it may feel too small.

Are there a lot of families that live here?
There are, particularly on our [first] floor, which is great because in the winter the children can play together in the corridor. As you go higher up the building there are fewer families and more older people who are not so keen on children cycling up and down the corridor!

Do most people rent or own their apartments?
Most people own. Sometimes people come and rent for a bit to test out the building and see whether they like it before they buy. Recently, as the building has become more fashionable, people have started buying up apartments to use as second homes or to rent out as holiday homes.

Are there many opportunities to get to know the rest of the residents in the building?
Yes, it's like a village here. There's a school on the eighth floor for children aged between three and six, so you get to meet lots of other parents and children. Having the school so close and just being able to take the elevator to it is fantastic. It's also great if you are working a little late, for example you can ask your neighbours to pick up your children too – we all help each other out. There's also a small cinema which is run by the residents. There's a library which is run mainly by the older people who are retired, so have more time on their hands. Then there is the roof terrace, of course, and in the summer everyone hangs out there. But if you don't want to be social, that's okay too. Before we had children, we didn't know many people.

And the older residents, are they people who have been here for a long time?
Yes, a lot of them have been here from the start and there are some people who have lived here all their lives. Many of them have recently moved out, however. The building has had major renovation works over the last ten years, and although we don't have to pay the full cost it is still really expensive. Some of the older residents – who originally were social tenants but later bought their apartments – just couldn't afford it and had to leave. A lot of people also moved out after there was a big fire here. The building is a UNESCO historic monument so any work needs to be done properly, which makes things very expensive. The exterior of the building needs to

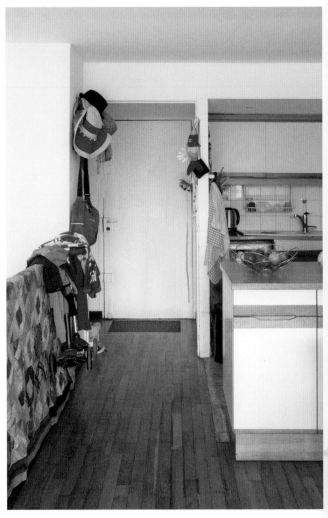

remain looking the same, such as the yellow outside our apartment, but inside you can pretty much do what you want. We don't have the original Charlotte Perriand kitchen, for example – it had already been replaced before we moved here.

Tell me about the fire

It was in 2012 and started in an apartment here on the first floor. I was pregnant with Ektor and at home. The woman who lived in the apartment was out, and we still don't know what started it. As there is so much wood in the apartments the fire spread really quickly, and the firemen took a long time to put it out so it spread to the neighbouring flats. We were all evacuated. When they finally managed to extinguish it we came back in, but then suddenly the fire spread to the fourth floor. Luckily, the fire brigade were still here, and they managed to put it out again. They didn't really know how the apartments were connected, and in particular that there are large voids between each of the flats for the pipes and cables etc., so the fire just went up. Ten apartments were

completely destroyed and a third of them had some kind of damage. Some people just didn't want to move back after that. We were lucky in that we weren't affected.

Have things improved now in terms of fire safety?

Very much so. We all have smoke detectors that are directly linked to the concierge downstairs and to the Marseille fire brigade, so as soon as the alarm goes off the concierge comes and checks it out.

And what about general maintenance of the building? What's included in your service charges?

Pretty much everything apart from electricity. Water, heating, cleaning of the common areas etc. For what you get, I don't think it's so expensive.

And how is the apartment heated?

There's hot air that blows out in each room. Some people complain that it's too cold, but in our apartment it's the opposite. It was breakthrough technology at the time, but it's getting quite old now.

What's the location like?

For me it's perfect as I work very close by. There's also everything you need, plenty of shops, so you don't need a car. We have a municipal park here, an area for children to play, and somewhere to grow vegetables. For a family with children, I think it is the best place to be.

Does it feel like you are living in an 'icon'?

I think there are a lot of people who move here because of the prestige of living in a Le Corbusier building, but I don't think they end up staying long. You have to really like the building to live here, it's getting old and some things don't work very well anymore. I don't think about it; maybe I did at first, but after twelve years here, for me it's just my home.

Opposite far left
View towards the double-height space, with the main bedroom below

Opposite left
View towards the kitchen and front door

Above
The main bedroom, looking towards the brise-soleil of the private balcony

Above
The children's bedroom. Originally there would
have been a sliding partition in the centre to divide
the space into two rooms

Opposite
The original built-in cupboards

Bloco das Águas Livres

Lisbon Portugal

Architects Nuno Teotónio Pereira and Bartolomeu Costa Cabral

In Portugal, during the time of the dictatorship of the Salazar regime, the recently completed housing scheme Bloco das Águas Livres symbolised a new modern future for Lisbon. The building was designed in 1953 by Nuno Teotónio Pereira (1922–2016) in collaboration with Bartolomeu Costa Cabral (b. 1929). It was funded by the Caixas de Previdência, a health insurance company, who at that time was the country's largest developer of non-profit housing. The scheme became one of the most emblematic of the principles of the Modern Movement in Portugal – it was in fact the first housing block of that style in the country.

Portguese-born Pereira had participated in the First National Congress of Architecture in 1948, affirming himself as one of the opponents of the aesthetics of the Salazar regime, namely against the idea of typical 'Portuguese architecture'. The country was turning its back to the outside world, but Pereira sought to present architectural designs that kept up with what was going on abroad, while maintaining Portuguese culture, history and identity. He was barely in his thirties when he began work on Bloco das Águas Livres.

The influence of Le Corbusier's Unité d'habitation is clear, but Bloco das Águas Livres, situated in the Rato area of Lisbon, surpasses strict functionalist principles. The building was designed for the modern city and for the modern family. Unlike the majority of mass housing in Europe of the time, the target audience was middle- to high-income families. Caixas de Previdência was committed to solving the housing shortage of Portugal, not only for the poorer classes but for the emerging middle classes, whose housing problems were also very real. Pereira was consultant for the insurance company and Cabral worked as its architect. The architect/client relationship was unique as no budget restraints were defined at the beginning of the project – they essentially had a blank cheque.

The quality of work and use of expensive materials including stone, plaster, mosaic, cork and iron can be seen throughout the building. The facade is of pink plaster, a traditional material used in Lisbon. A number of artists were commissioned to create artworks for the communal spaces, including a large bas relief, stained glass and stained concrete panels. The most striking artwork is a glazed mosaic in the large double-height lobby area by renowned Portuguese artist José de Almada Negreiros. The interiors of the apartments are spacious enough to accommodate families quite comfortably. In-built cupboards, washbasins and bespoke ironmongery were all specifically designed by the architects for the building. Ceiling, wall and floor colours were carefully considered – yellow, red and dark green are all used and achieve harmonious effect. There is also extensive use of glazing in the apartments, making them light and bright, and each has a generous balcony that acts as an extension to the living area, with spectacular views over the city. There are four apartment typologies, ranging from 95 to 185 square metres to allow for a diversity in family sizes. The building stands at twelve-storeys high, eight of which are for housing, with each residential floor having seven apartments of varying sizes, with a total of fifty-six dwellings.

As in the Unité, shops and offices are integrated into the building; however, here Pereira and Cabral did not raise the building on piloti, preferring instead to use the ground floor to house a parade of shops so that they integrate with the surrounding streets. Careful consideration was taken of how people would use the spaces in daily life. A floor is given to offices and the top floor to workshops and a party room for the residents. Further communal areas, such as laundry rooms and garages, are also provided. In 2012 the building was classified a monument of public interest.

Opposite
The Bloco das Águas Livres, shortly after completion

Pages 74–75
Double-height entrance lobby with mosaic by José de Almada Negreiros

José Pedro Croft

José is a renowned Portuguese painter and sculptor. Born in Porto, he moved to Lisbon as a child with his family and has lived there ever since.

How long have you lived here for and why did you choose to move here?

I bought the apartment in 2003. I think it is one of the most beautiful buildings in Lisbon, it's very special. Since it was built, in the 1950s, a number of interesting people have lived here – architects, actors, painters, historians. At that time this building, especially for conservative Portugal, was revolutionary. It was the first modern building with a community spirit. It took the principles of Le Corbusier's Cité Radieuse but humanised it, so the rooms are large and ceilings are high, for example, which it makes it very easy to live here.

What specifically do you like about the building?

The use of materials – it uses very pure and simple materials. Many of them were new and had not been used in domestic architecture before. It is a building where you don't need to have a lot of furniture, everything is integrated into the spaces, such as built-in cupboards. I also love the fact that it looks out to the sea and the landscape. The architecture brings the landscape into the apartment.

Was the building always aimed at creatives?

It's an interesting story. In Portugal, big insurance companies were obliged to provide some housing for rent. Usually they would renovate old buildings, but the architect Nuno Teotónio Pereira, the son of the CEO of an insurance company, persuaded his father to invest in a new building which he would design. It was after the Second World War and there was a longing for something new and a new way of living, which this building offered specifically for the upper-middle class (they were twice as expensive as others in the area) and the apartments were extremely popular.

Are some of those original residents still here?

There are only a few left, but my upstairs neighbour is one of the original residents. She's the widow of a famous actor.

And is it still expensive to live here?

The insurance company that owned the building tried to sell it to a Spanish insurance company some years ago, but the people who live here clubbed together and bought the building and their individual apartments. It is almost impossible to get an apartment here – when one comes up for sale, there are at least ten people that want it. I knew of a lady selling hers as she didn't need so much space, and although I'd never thought of buying somewhere before, when it came up for sale I worked hard to try to buy it.

Describe the layout of your apartment

There are five rooms: a large open plan living and dining room and four bedrooms. Then there is the kitchen and two bathrooms. There would have originally been three bathrooms, but I've knocked two together. There are also three balconies, each with a different aspect. It would originally have been for a family with three or four children and a maid.

Are there still families living here? What kind of people live here today?

All kinds – families, couples, people living on their own.

What was your apartment like when you bought it?

I had to completely renovate it, it didn't look anything like it does today. The previous owners had been here a long time and had transformed it in the 1970s to make it look like an eighteenth-century apartment! The hall floor was in marble, the doors were ornate with cast bronze door handles, the bathroom taps were in the shape of dolphins. They had even blocked up some of the windows as they thought the apartment was too bright! Working alongside the original architect, we took it back to how it used to be. I really enjoyed the experience of restoring it – I worked with fantastic people and skilled craftsmen, it was wonderful. I treated it in the same way as you might restore a painting.

The quality of the building and the materials is clearly evident in your apartment and in the communal areas

Yes, it's extraordinary, especially as the architects were

really young when they designed it and they essentially didn't have any financial restrictions. They could do what they liked using the best materials. The iron structure was imported from Germany, for example, and because they were such good materials they have lasted. The wooden floor in my apartment is original and the central boiler which heats the fifty or so apartments still functions.

What's the community like today, is there an opportunity to meet your neighbours?

There used to be a party space on the roof terrace, which had wonderful views of Lisbon, but that's not there anymore. But I know my neighbours – we go to each other's houses for dinner.

And the local area, what is that like?

We are in the Rato neighbourhood. When the building was built this would have been on the edge of Lisbon but now it's very central. It is also very well connected by transport.

What's the best thing about living here?

The notion of space, which is really important to me. The view of the sky, the river, the city, all of the hills. I have a room that I work from here, and I can see all of this from my window, it's just great. Even when it's raining, it looks fantastic.

Does the architecture affect the way you live?

Absolutely, when you wake up you are in a good mood. I just love it.

Above
The living room with full-height glazing leading to the balcony

Opposite
The dining area

Above left
The hallway with floor-to-ceiling built-in
cupboards, looking towards the bedrooms

Above right
Basin, which is located outside of the bedrooms,
reinstated to match the original design

Above
The kitchen (left), with door on the left-hand-side
which leads on to a covered balcony (right) that acts
as a clothes' drying area. There is a bedroom, originally
intended for the maid, next to the kitchen that also
has access to this balcony

Hansaviertel
Berlin
Germany

53 Architects including Oscar Niemeyer, Arne Jacobsen, Johannes Krahn, Alvar Aalto and Walter Gropius

By 1949 Germany had become two separate countries – the Federal Republic of Germany (West Germany) under Allied control, and the German Democratic Republic (East Germany) under Soviet control. Berlin was also a divided city and the eastern and western sides chose different approaches when it came to housing. Communist East Berlin's answer to urban development was monumental, decorated residential complexes, built for workers along Stalinallee (now Karl-Marx-Allee), heralded as the 'first socialist street' in Germany. In reaction, West Berlin decided to rebuild the area of Hansaviertel from scratch by reinstating the tradition of architectural exhibitions. The area on the edge of Berlin's Tiergarten had been heavily bombed during the Second World War.

An urban planning competition was announced in 1953 and the Allies and Federal Republic sponsored the show. The international housing competition, known as Interbau, was held in the summer of 1957 and presented a model of the 'city of tomorrow' in the International Style. It aimed to demonstrate the new democratic Western Germany to the outside world. The overall plan was managed by Otto Bartning, and the urban design competition was won by Gerhard Jobst and Willy Kreuer, whose plans were later executed in a modified form. Fifty-three internationally renowned architects were selected to design the buildings, including Oscar Niemeyer (1907–2012) from Brazil, Arne Jacobsen (1902–71) from Denmark, Johannes Krahn (1908–74) from Germany, Alvar Aalto (1898–1976) from Finland, and the German Bauhaus founder Walter Gropius (1883–1969).

Public parks were top priority and a zoological garden was integrated into the Hansa neighbourhood. Greenery was used to both separate and unify the urban elements and a mixture of high-rise and low-rise buildings were placed at the heart of the park landscape. The homes were intended as social housing, but the definition of those who were eligible was initially very broad, and in the early 1950s it included almost 70 per cent of the population. As well as housing, two churches, shops, restaurants, a theatre, library, kindergarten and an Academy of Arts building by Werner Düttmann (1921–83), the subway at Hansa Square was also incorporated across the 18-hectare site. Three additional buildings were erected outside the Hansaviertel area: Unité d'habitation designed by Le Corbusier, Congress Hall by Hugh Stubbins (1912–2006) and a primary school designed by Bruno Grimmek (1902–69).

The exhibition opened in the July of 1957 and during its three months' duration it received 1.4 million visitors. The scheme was only partly completed by that point, with only half of the 1,160 apartments finished. Attendees could visit each building site by taking specially built trams through the main exhibition area or by taking the funicular railway or even the cable cars that loomed over the district, so you could get a bird's-eye view of the whole area. The remaining buildings were completed by 1960.

The entire collection of buildings and gardens received protected landmark status in 1995.

Opposite
The cable cars which operated during the Interbau exhibition at Hansaviertel in 1957

Pages 84–85
Houses designed by Arne Jacobsen

Pages 86–87
The eight-storey building designed by Oscar Niemeyer

Andreas Schmolka and Birgit Wilshaus

Andreas and Birgit have recently retired. Andreas is a former lawyer and Birgit a linguist and bookseller. They live in a single-storey house designed by Johannes Krahn.

When did you move to Hansaviertel?
[B] We bought the house about twenty years ago.

Is it common to buy properties, as opposed to rent, in Germany?
[B] In Berlin most people rent – especially in flats. Hansaviertel was initially social housing, apart from the houses, but everything came on to the open market about twenty-five or thirty years ago. So now they are all privately owned, but many are still rented out.

Why did you choose to live here?
[B] I used to live in one of the blocks of flats here, about forty years ago. When Andreas used to come and visit me he would look down at this house and say one day he would like to own it. But it was a pipe dream, these houses never come on the market!

So how did you manage to buy it?
[B] The previous owner had had the house since it was built, and he was quite old. We heard from a mutual acquaintance that he had died and the house was up for sale. It was in quite a poor state internally, which put a lot of people off, I think. It took us nine months to negotiate the price, however.

Are they expensive?
[B] They were asking for quite a lot of money for it, but the house was in really bad shape. It was very old fashioned – the rooms were very small and everything was dark. We were lucky really as I think a lot of people who were interested in buying the house couldn't imagine living here because of the state of it. We had to renovate the whole house.

Is the architecture important to you?
[B] It was one of the reasons we bought the house, another was because we love the area. We are one of the few family houses in Berlin with access to the metro, which is just 50 metres away. It is really conveniently located, we are very close to the centre, the theatres, operas etc.

Has the area changed much in the twenty years since you bought the house?
[B] The demographic has changed quite a lot. It used to be mainly people who had moved in when the housing was first built, but a lot of those original residents have passed away now. Younger people then moved in, and now many of them have had children.

What's the area like?
[B] There's a little shopping centre, a library and we are very close to Zoo station.

Do you have to pay any maintenance for the common areas?
[B] We don't because we are just responsible for our house and garden. The blocks of flats have facility managers, and of course they have to pay for that.
[A] There's a residents' group that get together to discuss ideas on how to improve things in the area.
[B] Yes, for example, the shopping centre became quite run down recently so they are trying to do something about that.

I guess as they are over sixty years old, the buildings are showing signs of age?
[A] Yes, but Hansaviertel is listed, which means you can apply for money from the state for the upkeep of the buildings.
[B] That only applies to the exterior, though. We are in a Conservation Area, which means although you can do what you like to the inside, the outside needs to remain the same.

I imagine the area attracts a lot of architects that want to live here?
[A] A typical family is perhaps an architect and a teacher with two children. Some people, however, who have lived here for a long time – like our next-door neighbour – have no interest in the architecture and don't understand what all the fuss is about.

What is it about the architecture that you like?
[A] It's not decorative. It's very clean. Simple.

And it functions for you?
[A] We modernised the house when we moved in twenty years ago, so everything works. But it's too small. Everything is too small for today. Back in 1957, it was originally designed for a family with four children and their grandparents! Initially it had three small bedrooms, but we have opened them up to make one large kitchen.

So have you completely reorganised the layout?
[A] Not really, just the kitchen. The original kitchen would have been near the entrance; we have replaced it with a second bathroom. But the living room and our bedroom are where they have always been.

What's the best thing about living here?
[A] Location, location, location!
[B] You are surrounded by greenery — you are literally living in a park. For families with kids it's great, it is so close to everything. The lovely thing about our house is the light. We are the only house with windows looking out on to the street, all the others look into their own garden. We often look up from washing up or whatever and there's a group of architecture students peering in!

What's the worst thing about living here?
[B] Recently there's been an increase in the number of homeless people and refugees in the area. Our metro station is one of three in Berlin that is open all night for the homeless, which is good, but it has become a bit overwhelming. There's a twenty-four hour shop nearby that sells alcohol and that attracts a lot of people.

But does it feel like a safe place to live?
[A] Yes, yes…
[B] Some neighbours have started to feel less safe. There are a lot of older women that live here, and they have expressed concern. Some families with kids have also said the metro is not as nice as it used to be. Personally, I think it's a bit of an overreaction.

Do you imagine ever moving away from here?
[A] For me this is the perfect spot.
[B] When we bought this house I said to my father,
'The house is even good for when we get old as
there's no stairs!' Which he found very funny as I was
so young then.

**What's the general perception of this style of
architecture in Berlin – is it fashionable?**
[B] I think it is becoming a lot more fashionable, people
are beginning to move here for the architecture. But if
you're a young person and want trendy bars or cafes,
then this is not really the best area for that.
[A] That's the difference between this and the trendiest
areas of Berlin. There everyone speaks English, here
they speak German. What I like about it is that we have
a mixture of people – well-educated, such as doctors
and architects, as well as working class, and all sorts of
ages. I think this mixture is very, very nice.

Opposite far left
Exterior view of a house designed
by Johannes Krahn

Opposite left
The entrance lobby

Above
The living room which looks on to
an internal garden

Above left
View from the living room towards
the bathroom, which originally housed
the kitchen

Above right
The hallway

Above
The kitchen, originally two small
bedrooms and a playroom

Siedlung Halen

Bern Switzerland

Architects Atelier 5

In the early 1950s five young architects — Erwin Fritz (1927–92), Rolf Hesterberg (b. 1927), Samuel Gerber (1932–98), Hans Hostettler (b. 1925) and Alfredo Pini (b. 1932) — had the idea of designing and building five family houses for their own occupation. In 1955 they formed the architecture practice Atelier 5 and found a suitable plot to build on a few kilometres from Bern's city centre — a clearing in the middle of municipal woods overlooking the Aare River. It soon became apparent, however, that due to financial constraints building just five houses on the site would not be viable. The idea was abandoned in favour of a housing scheme that would accommodate the maximum amount of residents. Atelier 5 managed to gain funding for the Halen project of seventy-nine dwellings on the proviso that they would be personally responsible for finding buyers for the houses.

In the aftermath of the Second World War, Switzerland had experienced a period of stagnation with regards to modern housing, and not since the 1932 project of Neubühl in Zurich (see page 23) had the design of modern family housing been addressed. In Halen, many of the theories of the early Modernist Movement are evident, such as community and privacy, notions of a healthy lifestyle in a suburban setting and the considered use of materials and standardisation. Atelier 5 sought to offer high-density urban housing in a rural setting where cost, density of population and quality of life were all equally balanced.

The scheme is built on a sloping site and reminiscent of Le Corbusier's unrealised low-rise row schemes of 1948/49 at La Saunte-Baume and Roq et Rob in the South of France. The architects have also cited the narrow courtyard houses of medieval Bern as their inspiration. The long narrow houses in Halen are arranged in two parallel rows that are shifted slightly to create a larger landscaped public piazza. House types range from studios to seven-room dwellings, with most of the houses economically organised on three storeys. Due to the slope of the site, the dwellings are entered on the middle level (via a courtyard) which houses the kitchen, living space and a terrace at the back overlooking the forest. The space is divided by a steep staircase which leads up to the bedrooms, a bathroom and a small balcony and down to a multi-purpose space that can be used as extra bedrooms, a family room, studio or workspace. Distinct features of the houses include the green roofs and the balconies that act as a brise-soleil. Another innovative feature is that the interior walls are not structural. The architects believed the houses should be flexible, and internal spaces are designed to be easily reconfigured to suit the changing needs of a family.

Great importance was given to the differentiation between public, semi-public and private spaces. The houses all have outdoor spaces which are entirely private and separated by high walls with a cavity between each dwelling. The public paths and square on the estate serve as informal meeting points to enhance community and village life. This sense of community is reinforced further by the unique concept of co-operative ownership of the communal spaces. Each homeowner shares ownership of the swimming pool, garages, shop, cafe, petrol station, sports area and laundry as well as the surrounding area of woodland.

The scheme was completed in 1961. Two years after the estate was completed every house had finally been sold. The initial inhabitants were typically upper-middle class, well-educated and creative, and included many of the Atelier 5 architects, some of whom still live there today. Siedlung Halen immediately attracted the attention of the architectural press and today is widely regarded as the singularly most influential model of high-density, low-rise housing.

Opposite
Aerial view of Halen taken in 1963

Pages 96–97
View of the tops of the houses taken from the balcony of a neighbouring house

Page 98
The communal swimming pool

Page 99
Playing area in the Dorfplatz

Tim Prior
and Karin Büchler

Tim, who works at Switzerland's Federal Institute of Technology, is originally from Australia, and his wife Karin works at the Foundation for Swiss Youth in Science. They have two sons.

Describe your home
[T] We are in a row of houses which were originally designed by and for Atelier 5 architects. The house is set over three floors: on the top floor there's Karin's office, a bathroom and our bedroom which leads on to a sun terrace. On the middle floor is the kitchen, a large living room and another small balcony. On the lower floor there's the children's bedroom, another bathroom, some storage and a small garden at the back. We also have a courtyard at the front of the house.

What made you decide to live in Siedlung Halen and how long have you lived here for?
[K] My parents bought this house in 1969 – they were the second owners of it – so I grew up here until I was about thirteen years old. We then moved away to the countryside, just outside of Bern, but my family kept the house and decided to rent it out – so this house has been in our family for over forty years. I studied biology at Bern University, then went to Australia to do a PhD in marine science and that's where I met Tim. The plan was to stay there for two or three years then come back home – but I got stuck and it ended up being fourteen years and two children later! We moved back to Switzerland in January 2012 and lived in an apartment in Bern because this house was being rented out at the time. We moved here in 2013.

What was it like when you were growing up? Were there lots of families then? How does it compare to now?
[K] I thought living next to the forest was really normal then, but I remember the games that we had – a massive camp with Indian tents and big fires. It was pretty wild. There weren't as many children then as there are now. At the moment there are about fifty children living here. It's quite a unique environment for them to grow up in – there's a lot of freedom as they can roam around very independently because there's no traffic.

Are the houses privately owned or rented? How does it work?
[K] Both – some owners live in them, others are rented out. But all the common areas are owned by the owners.

Apart from the forest, what other communal areas are there?
[K] There's a grocery shop and just outside it is the Dorfplatz (village square), which is the main meeting point for the kids, where they bike, skate, play tennis and soccer. There's a swimming pool and next to it a sports field with ping pong tables, and there's a smaller area with swings and a barbecue. There's also a common laundry room. Quite a few people have put washing machines in their houses because they can't be bothered to carry everything down to it, but we decided not to because we have such little space and for us it really works.
[T] There's also a cafe area/meeting room, which anyone can use for birthday parties or events. We have our community meetings there every quarter where we decide on what work needs to be done to the Siedlung. For example, at the moment they are doing some work on the water pipes, so we will have to agree on that.

How does that work financially? Do you all have to put money towards the communal facilities?
[K] Yes, every month you put a certain amount towards a 'sinking fund'.
[T] The money goes towards the rubbish collection, heating, maintenance, and there's a caretaker that lives here too, so our funds pay for his salary. There was an interesting situation with the roofs recently. Because they are over fifty years old, some were leaking, but in order to make them waterproof they needed to be replaced as a single element, i.e. the whole row of houses.
[K] … and because not everyone had the money or was in agreement to have their roof fixed, the project was put on hold. It was done eventually, but it took over five years.

Did the fact that the estate is listed slow things down?
[K] It's been listed for a long time, but initially there

were no detailed regulations as to what you could and couldn't do to the buildings – that's why they all look so different. When they started this whole thing with the roof it brought up all these questions resulting in extensive guidelines, down to every little detail. Now if you want to do anything you have to make a formal request.

[T] For instance our neighbour two doors down has his courtyard covered with a glass roof, and it was leaking and needed renovating – but he had to wait three years or so until it was approved.

[K] When we moved back here in 2013 we needed to renovate the kitchen and the windows because they were all original and old. At that point they hadn't finished the guidelines and we were told we would have to wait until they were ready before we could do the work. But I told them that we had a family and we couldn't wait six months until the guidelines were finished, and they backed off, so we were lucky. It's a bit of a shame now, I'm not even sure you could take the kitchen out like we did.

I guess as everything is getting old it's becoming a problem as people need to do work on their homes?
[K] Yes, the whole electrical system and heating is really becoming a bit of an issue. Two houses in the last year have had their hot water pipes burst. The generation that lived in the Siedlung before us didn't do a lot of maintenance – they kind of let it go.

In terms of new people that are living here, do you think they are moving here because of the architecture? What kind of people live here?
[K] I think it's mixed but it's very hard to get a place here – unless you know someone – because it's all word of mouth. It's super family friendly, but if I hadn't grown up here I wouldn't have known that, and I think the architecture probably would have put me off. You are really all on top of one another, but the ingenious thing about the building is that it's built in a way that you can have your privacy. I can walk around naked everywhere and no one sees you, but outside your home it is very sociable – it can take forty-five minutes to come up here from the garage as you bump into people on the way.

[T] In this row of houses there are a lot of people our age. It's really nice – for example, last weekend we went to the mountains and hired a cabin with three neighbouring families. We actually first moved to Halen in 2008 but moved back to Australia soon after as I couldn't find a job. The population in the Siedlung was very different then. There was really only one other family with children the same age as ours. There were a lot of older people that had lived here for thirty or forty years. When we came back in 2013 a lot of those older people had moved out, and their children moved back in to take over the houses, but I think it's really important that we have older people here too because that makes for a real population. If you have all young people or all old people, then that's not a real community.

Do you think the architecture helps form that community?
[K] I totally think so. Everybody's door is open here, kids go from house to house – they are living with pretty much ten different families. For us, we can go up to the pool when everyone is there, you chat for a while – it's totally fluid. I think if you live somewhere more separated, every time you have someone over you would feel like, 'Oh I have to clean up my house, make it nice', but because everyone's door is open here, you can't do that – it's intimate, almost. People come in when you are still in your pyjamas and your house might be in a mess, but it doesn't matter – everyone has a family and mess!

Is it expensive to live here?
[K] Yes, definitely, I think so. The majority of people here are architects, doctors, well-established creatives. It's not a low budget place to live.
[T] The underlying costs of living in Switzerland are generally very high whether you are living here or in a house down the road. I guess one of the big costs we have here is the maintenance.

What's the location and area like?
[K] The immediate surroundings are a bit isolated because of the forest but again, that's brilliant for the kids. There's a bus that takes you to the city which takes about ten minutes and it's also whithin cycling distance.

[T] Every morning I ride up to the train station to go to Zurich – there's a road that runs directly through the forest and takes me right into the university street which goes to the station. I can be there in twelve minutes.

When you first saw this place, Tim, what did you think of it?
[T] My first and persisting thought was that it's very grey. The concrete is quite heavy. For the most part, from October until February, it's grey and dark. It's really interesting how the life of the community changes very dramatically with the seasons. In the summer it's a completely different place. Everyone is out all the time on the Dorfplatz having a beer, or we're having a barbecue or everyone is at the pool. In winter you close off – it's like hibernation, essentially.

What is the general perception of this place?
[K] It's mixed, but I have friends who come here and think it's horrible. There are other people that think it's like a Greek holiday resort! When people visit us, they often think, 'Oh my goodness, this is a tiny space,' but the whole surrounding area is also our home.
[T] I think it's hard for people who don't live here to gauge what it's actually like. Coming from Australia, my life in Switzerland would be very different if we lived somewhere else. We have such good friends and relationships with the people here – if we had moved to a big house out in the countryside I wouldn't have met anyone.

Do you think if you hadn't inherited this you would still want to live here?
[K] I think it's unlikely that we would be here because I wouldn't have even known about it. I think if we would have come here and looked at the house, I would have got the impression that it is very concrete – but for this stage of our lives, with our young kids, I think it's absolutely perfect.

Page 103
The kitchen, looking towards the front courtyard

Opposite
View from the living room towards the staircase
and the kitchen beyond

Above
Living room with full-width glazing opening to
a private balcony, with characteristic brise-soleil

Above right
The main bedroom situated on the first floor

Above left
The children's bedroom on the lower
ground floor

Opposite
Looking towards the garden from the
children's bedroom

Calthorpe Estate

Edgbaston Birmingham England

Architect John Madin

Much of the rebuilding of the UK's towns and cities following the Second World War was undertaken by the government and local councils. Although there was an acute shortage of housing for the working classes and much of the existing Victorian housing stock was inadequate, there was also a need for affordable housing for middle-class families. Local councils encouraged private developers to build homes – often by offering them subsidies to do so. Eric Lyons and his company Span Developments were one of the most successful in designing and supplying private modern homes for post-war Britons in the south of England. In Birmingham, there was also a quiet revolution of modern house building, led by architect John Madin (1924–2012).

Birmingham-born Madin visited Stockholm in 1949 and thought its humanist housing schemes exemplary, so he took many of the ideas back with him to England. One of his first major architectural projects was an office building in Edgbaston, a leafy south-western suburb of Birmingham. In 1957, the success of the building led the Calthorpe Estate (which owned much of the land in Edgbaston) to commission a masterplan for the area. Madin was later made chief architect of the whole estate. The 1,600-acre site owned by Lord Calthorpe had been home to spacious Victorian villas. After the war these large houses had become uneconomical; the estate wanted to increase its commercial revenue and attract middle-class families and single residents, without compromising on the character of the area.

Madin strongly believed that no new building should be erected until it could be shown to fit in with the surrounding area and that planning should be considered as a whole. For the Calthorpe Estate, Madin's solution was to assign a third of the area to buildings, a third to landscaping and the last third to car parking. The buildings, not dissimilar in style to those of Span Developments, comprise a mix of low-rise apartment blocks, terrace housing and a single tall block of flats among rich planting, as well as some commercial buildings. Most of the buildings built between 1958 and 1973 were produced for Artizan/Vista Developments, a subsidiary of the Calthorpe Estate.

Madin managed to raise the density of the area in line with the rest of the city in such an unobtrusive manner that the change was hardly noticed. His skill in incorporating buildings into the existing landscape of mature trees won him an award from the Ministry of Housing and Local Government in 1964 for his buildings on Cala Drive and Estria Road. Built between 1959 and 1962, the two cul-de-sacs are in the shape of an L, and comprise detached houses, terraces and two-storey blocks of flats. The townhouses, known as Integro, feature first-floor balconies forming canopies to the front doors below. They are clad in grey buff brick with dark hexagonal tile hanging and horizontal white timber weather boarding.

As well as housing, Madin was responsible for many other buildings in Birmingham, including the city's Central Library, which was demolished in 2016 despite a strong public campaign to save it, and Pebble Mill television studios.

Opposite
Cala Drive, 1962

Pages 110–111
The houses today at Estria Road

Mary Keating

Mary, a social worker, lives in a house on Estria Road. She represents the Brutiful Brum group, which campaigns to save Birmingham's Brutalist landmarks.

How long have you lived here?
It's coming up to six years. I used to live in Edgbaston some years ago but when I had my daughter we moved to one of Birmingham's suburbs. When she went off to university I knew I wanted to come back.

What was it about Estria Road that you liked?
I came across Estria Road by chance – even though you might pass it every day, you'd never know it was here. I just fell in love with the whole development. It took me a long time to sell my previous home and I would obsess about every house that came on to the market. I just knew I wanted to live here – you can walk into the city in twenty minutes, but as soon as you walk into the drive it's like flicking a switch and you are in the middle of the countryside. You can't hear anything apart from the birds twittering.

What were your first impressions when you came to see the house?
What a fabulous floor! I loved the living room and being able to see straight into the garden, I liked the generous size of the hallway. I'd been looking at Victorian conversions before this and those spaces always seemed compromised and narrow. This house is very bright and airy.

Are the houses sought after?
They are, but it's mainly due to the location. Edgbaston is one of the nicest areas in Birmingham and small houses are hard to come by.

They were designed as family houses – are there still a lot of families that live here?
At the moment there's a lot of retired single women here. There are three young families that live in my part of the development. The problem is that there's a lack of good secondary schools here – unless you are going to pay for it. So young families move here but soon move out.

Was it easy to integrate yourself into the local community?
Absolutely. I had never lived in a cul-de-sac before but I've made a lot of friends here, everyone is very nice.

I noticed Estria Road is a private road. Who is in charge of maintaining it?
We have a managing agent. We pay quite a chunk of money for the service charges every month, which covers the grounds, the paths, lights and garages. Part of the contract is that they paint all the houses every so often and although they don't always do them all that well (so there is some anger about the cost), it does mean that they are all uniform in colour, which I think is really important.

Have many people tried to alter their exteriors?
Oh yes, lots of the original balconies have gone, especially in Cala Drive, the road further up. It has almost been ruined – virtually all their balconies have gone and people have built out. I don't think that would be allowed now as it's in a conservation area.

Is the house easy to maintain?
Before I moved in I had a number of things done to the house, such as plumbing, electrics and a new kitchen, but I didn't do anything with the windows. It's quite a cold house so this year I had all the windows on the front repaired – that was quite a major job. It's important for me to maintain the integrity of the design, such as the original Crittall windows, so I had double glazed units installed into the original frames.

Was it living here that got you interested in the architecture?
It was only after I had moved in that I realised it was designed by the same architect as Birmingham's Central Library. I joined the Friends of the Library to try and save it from being demolished, I then joined the Twentieth Century Society and got involved in the West Midlands group – and it snowballed from there. I was asked whether I would open up my house for Open House weekend about three years ago and to my surprise I was inundated with visitors.

Are there any shops that were integrated into the development?

Part of John Madin's original plan was that there would be shops in both the east and west side. Over the road there's Templefield Square where there are a few shops but they change hands quite frequently. The Calthorpe Residents Society are trying to create more community hubs and have recently opened a community art gallery/cafe in the square, which I think is great.

What's the best thing about living here?

The location and the garden. I spend a lot of time just looking out of the windows. It's just an easy place to be.

Above left
View from the entrance hall

Above right
The dining area, with the kitchen beyond

Opposite
The living room looking towards the garden

Above left
The main bedroom viewed from the landing

Above right
Looking towards the landing and the second bedroom

Opposite
The hallway with original parquet flooring

Tanto
Stockholm
Sweden

Architects
Åke Ahlström
and
Kell Åström

Designed by Swedish architects Åke Ahlström (1918–2001) and Kell Åström (1920–2004), the housing at Tanto on the Stockholm island of Söder is a fine example of high-quality, well-planned slab block design. In 1956 the architects created an overall masterplan for the undeveloped area which belonged to a former sugar factory – Svenska Sockerfabriks AB (later AB Cardo). The plan was approved by the City of Stockholm and Ahlström and Åström, commissioned by the sugar company, went on to design the buildings for the site.

Roughly triangular in plan and on the edge of the island, the site is surrounded by the South General Hospital (one of the largest in Stockholm) on one side, the railway line on another and water on the other. The scheme comprises five curved buildings of varying height, staggered on a sloping site. Towards the back and at the top of the slope near the railway line is the tallest buildings at fifteen storeys, which acts as an acoustic barrier, and at the front are the shortest blocks, which stand at nine storeys. The curve of the blocks cleverly allows the apartments to catch the maximum amount of sunlight during the day. The fronts face towards the water, making the most of the views, with the backs of the buildings facing towards the railway line. The curve is produced by putting together a series of wedge-shaped staircase sections.

What distinguishes the buildings at Tanto from later developments built during the 'Million Homes Programme' in Sweden, is the sheer level of quality materials, fittings and finishes used, such as the double-glazed windows and the black-glazed tiles on the facade. There are a total of 729 apartments, which vary in size from studios to five-room family dwellings, for over 1,200 people. Commercial units are placed on the ground floor.

Internally, the apartments are of an equally high standard. Originally kitchens came fully equipped with stainless steel double sinks, electric cookers, built-in fridge freezers and plenty of built-in cupboards. Bathrooms were fully tiled with baths as well as hand-held showers, and with enough room for a washing machine. There was also plenty of storage and built-in wardrobes in the bedrooms. Communal facilities included a laundry room in the basement, bicycle storage and individual tenant store rooms.

The whole scheme is essentially car-free with underground car parking or spaces on the periphery of the estate. Between the buildings are a series of landscaped formal gardens with concrete retaining walls repeating the shapes of the buildings. At the centre is a park with rocky outcrops and mature trees, and pedestrian routes that lead to each block.

Construction was quick, due to the innovative building methods, which included a series of in-situ concrete crosswalls and floor slabs that were craned and placed in position floor by floor, plus the use of drywall partitions that did not need plastering. The larger blocks took only a year and a half to build and the smaller ones a year. Three cranes per block were used, with no need for scaffolding.

The scheme was completed in 1965. The sugar company owned and managed the estate until 1980. Following proposals from the residents, the houses were bought by HSB (Sweden's largest housing co-operative) and the Tanto housing association was formed. Today, of 729 apartments, around 100 are still rental properties.

Opposite
Construction of the Tanto
buildings, 1964

Pages 120–121
The buildings today viewed from
the top of the sloping site

Helena Ekelund

Helena and her partner Aksel, both architects, live in a two bedroom apartment on the eighth floor with their two young children.

How long have you lived here for?
We moved to Södermalm about nine years ago and initially rented an apartment in the centre. Before that I used to live in a small 1930s apartment in central Stockholm, which was in a great location, but most of my friends were living in Södermalm. It's the trendier part of Stockholm, there are lots of creative people, so we decided to look at buying an apartment here. We would have liked to stay in the centre of Södermalm, but it's expensive and we wouldn't have been able to afford a three-room apartment, which we wanted as we were thinking of starting a family. We knew some people living here in Tanto, so we decided to check it out and we really liked it. We've been in this apartment for six years.

What was it about it you liked?
We had a wish list of things we wanted in a flat – practical things like being able to fit a dishwasher, a washing machine, having a bathtub, a good view, car parking space – this apartment ticked every box. A lot of the older apartments we looked at felt compromised in their layout – bathrooms, for example, are often squeezed into hallways, as originally bathrooms were located in the basement of buildings.

Do most people in the building own their flats?
Yes, almost everybody. Initially all the flats were rental, but then the building was sold off and people were able to buy their apartments. It works as a co-op, so we all own a percentage of the entire building.

And how does that work in terms of managing the building?
We pay a fee towards the general maintenance – for the people who run the office, the landscaping, parking etc. and towards any costs for future major works. It works very well.

Is it difficult to find a flat to buy here?
Yes, in Sweden when you sell a property the estate agent holds an 'open house' for a day or two. Say that's on a Saturday, by the Tuesday the property will probably already have been sold. We were initially going to buy a flat here on the third floor but were outbid. Eventually this one came on to the market; it had only ever had one previous owner, so it was all original and hadn't been messed about with. As architects, the original features are really important to us. When we came to view it, we fell in love with it straight away and managed to get it for less than the other one was sold for, so it worked out perfectly.

So the apartments are desirable?
They didn't used to be, but it's getting much more that way. A friend of mine moved here in the early 2000s and I remember thinking at the time, 'Why would you live there?' It felt like a suburb. Now I see it very differently. The view is incredible and you can't really get that anywhere else in Stockholm unless you pay a lot of money. For me it's the urban dream – you are still in the city but connected to nature, and have the practicalities like car parking, and somewhere for the kids to play.

What's the area like?
In the immediate area there aren't as many restaurants or bars as there are in the centre of Södermalm, which is a shame, it would be nice to have somewhere really close to go to with the children. We have a small convenience store but that's pretty much it.

Is there a good community here?
A lot of my friends say they don't spend time with their neighbours, but here it's different. Everyone is very friendly, we get together on Saturday evenings, or meet up outside by the children's playground. There are a lot of families like us, also a lot of architects, of course, and graphic designers, journalists. We are similar in that many of us have studied for a long time but don't necessarily have huge incomes. I think bankers or lawyers, for example, wouldn't want to live in this kind of building.

What other communal spaces are there?
There is a gym, a sauna, two or three different spaces that you can use for parties, and a carpentry workshop.

There are also three guest apartments that you can rent out to friends or family who come to stay, which is fantastic. They are very reasonably priced, but they make quite a good income for the co-op.

The buildings are over fifty years old, are they beginning to show signs of age?

The pipes are terrible! Nearly everybody in the building has had a problem with leaking pipes, and everyone has a dehumidifier on standby just in case. Early next year, though, we are going to have all new pipes fitted throughout the building, which is a massive project. It will take about two months in each flat and means taking our entire bathroom out – the whole project will take a couple of years.

In general, how is 1960s concrete architecture viewed in Sweden?

These buildings were completed in 1964 or so and the quality is very good. You can see it in the use of materials such as the timber windows and the tiling on the facade. A few years later the Swedish government embarked on the 'Miljonprogrammet', a programme to build a million homes at a reasonable price to tackle the shortage of decent accommodation. Some people are critical of those buildings as they are perceived as uniform and not of such good architecture and quality.

Tall buildings are often criticised for not being suitable for families. How is living on the eighth floor working for your family?

It works perfectly for us. It's no different to living on the second or third floor. We have a large elevator, so you can just push your pushchair in and take it straight to your flat. It's very easy. Sometimes we consider the possibility of moving further out and getting a house but you can't beat this area. I love the connection to the water here, and if you cross the bridge you are in the forest. I ride my bike everywhere and it only takes me twenty minutes to get to work. If I pop downstairs in the elevator I always meet someone I know and have a chat, it's such a great community. Life here is very good.

Opposite
The living room

Above
Looking towards the main bedroom

Opposite
The kitchen looking through towards
the dining area

Above left
The main bedroom

Above right
The children's bedroom

Cables
Wynd House
and
Linksview House

Leith
Edinburgh
Scotland

Architects
Alison &
Hutchison &
Partners

Throughout the nineteenth and the beginning of the twentieth century, housing in Scotland's cities was seriously inadequate. Slum housing saw people in overcrowded, damp and unhygienic living conditions. Whole families often lived in just one room and the lack of sanitary facilities led to the spread of diseases such as cholera, typhus and tuberculosis. The Second World War only confounded the problem and by the mid-1940s serious action had to be taken. The building of quality council homes became a priority and the Government Programme for Scotland called for 50,000 homes to be built a year. The crisis was partly solved by the garden city and later new town movement, with self-contained communities being built out of towns. However, this was not enough to ease the pressure on urban inner cities.

During the 1960s the problem of poor housing continued, which led to local councils focusing on building high-density, high-rise mass housing. Glasgow, whose housing problems were most acute, dominated the Scottish debate and a number of high-rise developments, such as the Red Road flats (now demolished) and Basil Spence's Hutchesontown C (also demolished) were erected. Edinburgh Burgh Council was also fully committed to rehousing the city's working classes and the Kirkgate area in Leith, north of Edinburgh, is an example of such 1960s slum clearance and redevelopment.

The buildings in Kirkgate were designed by Alison & Hutchison & Partners, with Robert Forbes Hutchison (1908–76) as the senior partner and Walter Scott (1926–2010) as partner in charge. Cables Wynd House, commonly referred to as the 'Banana Flats', was built between 1963 and 1965 and is an elongated ten-storey slab block – the largest in Europe at that time. Its companion slab block, Linksview House, was built a little later between 1964 and 1967 and also stands ten storeys high.

The design and concept of the buildings was very much inspired by the ideas of Le Corbusier and his Unité d'habitation. Characterising the New Brutalism, it uses concrete for both aesthetic and practical reasons – for example, the use of a concrete crosswall method meant balconies could be recessed within the contour of the building. Both buildings are constructed with an in-situ concrete cross frame with large aggregate pre-cast concrete panel cladding. Cables Wynd House contains 212 flats and Linksview House has ninety-five. The apartments are accessed by lifts leading to galleried decks on the second, fifth and eighth floors.

Internally, the apartments offered 'all mod cons'. For families that had come from slums with no bath or inside toilet, conveniences such as underfloor heating, bathrooms, lifts and a modern refuse-shoot system must have seemed a luxury.

As early as the 1970s, however, the reputation of such estates went downhill and the backlash against Brutalism ensued. Lack of maintenance and social problems saw a rejection of this whole period of housing and great swathes of high-rises have been demolished in recent times, particularly in Glasgow, eradicating a whole period of architectural history. Cables Wynd House and Linksview House, however, were given the highest level of protection in 2017 when they were awarded Category A status by Historic Environment Scotland. The buildings were said to be among the best examples of quality 1960s social housing schemes.

Opposite
Cables Wynd House in the 1960s

Page 130
Linksview House today

Page 131
Deck access at Linksview House

Robert Peacock
and Jo Petey

Robert works for a palliative care charity and Jo runs her own painting and decorating company. They live in a two-bedroom apartment in Linksview House, and have recently had their first daughter.

As neither of you are from Scotland, how did you come to be living in Leith?

[R] I'm from Bradford originally. I went to university here and since graduating in 2000 always wanted to move back. In 2013, when I was made redundant from my last job, I decided to come back and that's when I met Jo.
[J] I'm originally from Wales, but I've lived in Edinburgh for seventeen years. When I first moved here I got myself on the Housing Association waiting list and managed to get a tiny flat in Leith in an old tenement building.

So how come you are living in Linksview House now?

[J] Rob moved in with me to the old flat, but it was tiny. We swapped that flat with the guy who was living here – he wanted to downsize and we wanted more space to possibly have a family.

When you say swapped, how does that work?

[J] There is a council list that tells you which properties are available, and you can search to see if there are any eligible for a direct swap. We wanted to stay in Leith. When I saw this flat come up I wasn't so sure at first because the estate has a bit of a reputation, but we thought it was worthwhile checking it out as the location is great.

And what did you think of it when you came to see it?

[J] We thought, 'Wow'. It's really well designed, it feels really big, and the views are fantastic. We thought it would be perfect for us. We just got great a vibe from it.

Describe your flat

[R] You come through the front door and down a set of stairs into a hallway. Off the hallway are two bedrooms, the bathroom and the living room. Off the living room there's a kitchen with a glass partition that you can look through. There's also a balcony, which isn't that deep, but runs the full width of the flat, so a lot of light comes into the flat.

You mentioned the building has a reputation – what kind of reputation?

[J] Just a bit rough, basically – drugs, fights – but it's not as bad as people make out. Everyone is very friendly and says hello in the stairwells. We have a concierge that really cares about his job and that really helps. He is always cleaning the place; if there's a little bit of graffiti, for example, he's out there scrubbing it clean. There's quite a few vulnerable people living here and people with all kinds of problems, but he knows and keeps an eye out for everyone.

Is there a mixture of people living here?

[J] Yes, it's very diverse – all sorts of nationalities, and I think there are quite a few refugees. That's the great thing about living here, there's more diversity here than in the rest of Edinburgh.

And is it mainly council tenants, as opposed to owners, here?

[J] There is a couple that I've met that own and they must have bought their flat through the Right-to-Buy scheme, but the majority are still council tenants.

Is there much of a difference in terms of the way the council maintains this building compared to your experience with a Housing Association?

[J] There's definitely a difference. Housing Associations are more on top of things when it comes to repairs, and the quality of the work they do is better.
[R] Our door had been kicked in and was pretty much hanging off its hinges when we moved in, and the council took months to replace it.

What do your family and friends think of the building and the style of the architecture?

[J] Initially I think there were a few raised eyebrows.
[R] You make certain assumptions from the exterior of the building, but when you come inside you realise how great it is. The building was Grade A listed earlier this year, and we went to the consultation. There weren't many residents there apart from us. There are so many places like this that have been demolished recently, I think there was a feeling that we need to retain this one

while we still can. We were in support of the listing but a lot of people were opposed to it. Many people think it's an eyesore and should be ripped down.

Had you lived in a post-war flat before?

[R] Growing up in Yorkshire some of my older relatives lived in high-rises and I remember going to visit them. It was quite exciting – going to the top of the building and seeing the whole of the town.

[J] I grew up in the sticks in Wales and there was nothing like this there. I'd never thought about making a beeline for this kind of architecture, but the more time we spend here, the more we love it. There are not many original features left, but the layout is far more generous than in a new build. They actually thought about families living here, as opposed to just putting you in a shoebox. It's also really well built – the walls and floors are very solid

What's Leith like as an area?

[R] It's really interesting as it's changed a lot in the last twenty years. It used to be quite rough. When I was at university here, I worked in a betting shop, and I remember not feeling that safe walking about. The main road, Leith Walk, that goes to Edinburgh, used to have an 'old man's pub' on every corner and now about half of those have been turned into craft beer pubs.

[J] Ten or fifteen years ago there would have been prostitutes on the streets near the docks; now it's full of bars and cafes. Probably for a lot of Leithers and people living in this building, it's all got too expensive for them.

Is that because younger people are moving here?

[R] It's that classic thing, as it's a cheaper part of town a lot of creative people moved here, so it got a reputation for being a creative area, but with a bit of an 'edge'.

Have you seen much of a change in the type of people moving to this building?

[J] As it's mainly council tenants here and it's so hard to get a flat in the first place, not really. That's why we feel so lucky and grateful to have a home here. We like the community as it is – the good and the bad bits.

Page 134 left
The living/dining room, with kitchen to the right

Page 134 right
The hallway with stairs leading up to the front door

Page 135
The two bedrooms viewed from the hallway

Above left
Original built-in bookcase between kitchen and living room

Above right
Looking towards the balcony from the living room

Opposite
The private balcony

Ivry-sur-Seine

Paris
France

Architect
Jean Renaudie

The work of architect Jean Renaudie (1925–81) in the 1960s and 70s can be seen as a reaction against the 'grands ensembles' schemes that swept across France from the 1950s. The state-run programme sought to solve the country's housing shortage by building mass housing in the form of standardised slab blocks, built in batches of 4,000 units or more in place of industrial slums.

Ivry-sur-Seine, a south-eastern suburb of Paris, had been building good quality, pioneering social housing since the beginning of the twentieth century, and politically demonstrated strong electoral support for the French Communist Party. With its population growing and its existing housing stock in poor condition, there came a need to build 2,400 dwellings with two-thirds designated for social rent.

In 1969 the then chief architect and urban planner of Ivry, Renée Gailhoustet, brought in Jean Renaudie to meet Raymonde Laluque, the young director of Ivry's Office of Public Housing. Renaudie, a Marxist and a member of the French Communist Party for most of his life, believed people had the right to unique and diverse dwellings with access to private outdoor space. He argued that cities were living organisms and should not be reduced to basic functions as promoted in the grands ensembles. He drew inspiration from philosophy to biology, mathematics to humanism, but rarely from architecture. For him, theory and architectural practice went hand in hand.

At the meeting with Laluque, Renaudie presented drawings from an unrealised housing project at Le Vaudreuil, France. These extraordinary abstract drawings – mostly fluid circles and doughnut shapes in coloured felt-tip pen – bore little resemblance to buildings. His radical approach was well received and Renaudie was commissioned to work on his first building at Ivry, Danielle Casanova, which housed eighty apartments and several shops.

The Casanova building, which acted as a blocks for his later schemes, could not be further from the monotonous towers of the grands ensembles. The building resembles a concrete mountain composed of stars and triangles, with each dwelling completely unique and having a large (almost a third of the apartment) triangular grassed terrace with overflowing greenery. The units are built on a 5 × 5 metre grid and are stacked on top of each other in a staggered manner so that each terrace is open to the sky. The complicated plans were being constantly adapted and the amendment of one unit would cause a chain reaction throughout the whole building.

Renaudie wanted to serve both the individual and the collective. The juxtaposition of buildings and the interface between the dwellings was designed to ensure the maximum amount of opportunity for social interaction between the inhabitants. For example, the underground car park has no access to the lift, so residents need to walk up a level to the elevator, therefore increasing the chance of bumping into a neighbour. Externally, the theme of triangles and diagonals is continued in the facade of Casanova, and exposed concrete is painted off-white in contrast with the colourful communal spaces of the lobbies and corridors.

In 1970 Renaudie was appointed joint chief architect of the urban renewal of Ivry along with Gailhoustet. Unusually, no masterplan was ever produced and the project grew in a piecemeal manner as a consequence of the ad-hoc acquirement of land. Danielle Casanova was completed in 1972 and several further buildings across the town followed, including Jean Hachette in 1975 with forty apartments and a commercial centre. Altogether, the redevelopment of Ivry included 1,700 dwellings designed over a period of two decades. In 1978 Renaudie was awarded the National Architecture Prize by the French Minister for Culture in recognition of his career.

Opposite
View of the Jeanne Hachette
mixed-use complex, taken in the 1970s

Pages 140–41
The Danielle Casanova building

Pages 142–43
View of Ivry from the terrace of an
apartment in Danielle Casanova

Elisabeth Huttier

A former type and image setter for a printing firm, eighty-five-year-old Elisabeth has three children and six grown-up grandchildren.

How long have you lived in Danielle Casanova?
I have lived here since the building was completed in 1972. Initially I lived in another apartment a couple of floors below but that one didn't have a balcony. A couple of years later I was told by the architect, Jean Renaudie, whose practice was on the ground floor of the building, that another apartment had become available. It was fantastic, plus it had the benefit of having a terrace.

When everybody first moved into the building, did the residents get a choice of which apartment they could have?
I think Renaudie would have liked that to have been the case, but it would have been too complicated, so we were assigned the apartments.

Did you know Jean Renaudie personally?
Not initially. I used to be childhood friends with his ex-wife, Renée Gailhoustet – the chief architect of Ivry-sue-Seine – and I met him through her some years later. Once the building was completed, Renaudie moved here too, including moving his atelier here, and so we became good friends.

Can you describe your apartment?
It's 85 square metres. Many of the apartments have an open plan kitchen but mine doesn't. I have turned one of the bedrooms into a large living space – Renaudie was keen for the residents to do what they wanted to the inside of the apartments, to be able change walls around etc. so that it would best suit them. Then there is my bedroom which leads to the large triangular terrace, there's a dining area, which also has access to the terrace, a small children's bedroom and a basic bathroom. My children really liked living in this apartment, it's very bright and comfortable to live in. Apart from a coat of paint, the flat is as it was when I moved in. It really needs renovating, but I will leave it for someone else to do!

How was the building received when it was first built?
Casanova was the first building to be completed; it has eighty apartments and not one of them was the same. Some people struggled with the concept – it was very unusual for social housing. Initially some people didn't want to move here and refused to, but with time it became a real success and gained international interest. Sociologists in particular were very interested in it and have studied how people live here.

What is the community like?
When we first moved in it was fantastic. Most of us had come from small apartments with no outdoor space. The terraces here played a really strong part in creating the community and in us getting to know each other. We didn't know how to garden and look after plants so we started a gardening group where we would share knowledge with each other, buy plants, and we all clubbed together to buy a single lawnmower that we shared. We were all a lot younger then and most of us had families and young children. We would leave our front doors open and our children would wander from one apartment to another. Renaudie placed great importance in neighbours interacting with each other, and the terraces really helped unite the community. We could be outdoors and chat to each other, but indoors is very private. It had a real village community. Interestingly, Renaudie purposefully didn't put lifts in the underground car parks – he wanted people to come out of the car and walk up a level, increasing the possibility of bumping into a neighbour.

And what is it like now?
In forty-six years it has changed. A lot of the original residents have passed away or moved out of Paris to the countryside. There is still a core group of us; we meet up and have dinner or water each other's terraces, but it's not the same as it used to be. It was a different time then, and there was more of a community spirit.

Do new people who move here find it difficult to integrate?
I usually go and introduce myself when someone new

moves in, but it doesn't usually go any further. People prefer to keep themselves to themselves these days. The newer generation don't really get the original utopian concept. I think people really like the apartments, but they are not interested in the history of the building. It's the same everywhere; I own a house in a village and it is the same there – people are only interested in the individual, times have changed.

Are you sad about those changes?
I am, but on my floor there is still a good feeling.

Are the apartments owned or tenanted?
They were built as social housing, and there is a strong council policy to keep them that way so that they are affordable for ordinary families. There are, however, seven apartments in another building that are artists' workshops which are available to buy, in fact my daughter lives in one which is fantastic – it has three terraces! A new law in France was introduced that meant councils could sell off some of their housing stock to

raise money, but in Ivry the Habitation à Loyer Modéré (Rent Controlled Housing) objected.

Are there any communal spaces where residents can meet?
Yes, there is a room for residents' meetings. The town has been Communist for a long time, and although things are changing, people are still interested in coming together and finding out what is happening in the local area, and there is still a strong sense of solidarity. There are also a lot of smaller organisations such as Le Hublot which started about twenty-five years ago – an art gallery where every week a different artist exhibits their work and every Friday evening they hold a private view. In the early days we could also go to the roof terrace, but that's locked now and you need a key to enter. There is also a communal terrace where people can grow fruit and vegetables.

Is the building well looked after?
No, the buildings have been really neglected. There

hasn't been any major renovation work done to them since they were built. The exterior concrete needs maintenance and the original windows, which are timber and single glazed, are all rotting. There is a programme planned to replace the windows in 2021 but the council wants to replace them with a cheaper version that is low maintenance, such as uPVC or aluminium. Those of us who care about the building feel really strongly that any replacement should be like for like.

Is the building protected at all?

It is in the process of being listed, but it's a complicated matter. I feel really strongly that the heritage of the building and the exceptional design really need to be protected. They are such fantastic apartments.

Opposite
The dining room, with sliding window on the right leading to the grassed terrace

Above left
View towards the terrace from the living room

Above right
The original kitchen

Above
View towards the dining room
from the entrance hallway

Above
View towards the entrance from the dining room

Above left
The main bedroom

Above right
View towards the bedroom from the terrace

Above
View towards the terrace

151

Monte Amiata Gallaratese II

Milan Italy

Architects Carlo Aymonino and Aldo Rossi

Situated on the north-west green belt of Milan, Gallaratese was part of Italy's answer to the chronic lack of affordable low-cost housing. The area had been marked out for development following the Second World War and in 1956 a masterplan was drawn up by the Rationalist architect Piero Bottoni, the Italian delegate to the International Congresses of Modern Architecture (CIAM) and a critical force behind the drafting of the Charter of Athens. The development would be completed in two phases, with the second given to Rome-based architect Carlo Aymonino (1926–2010) to design. He in turn commissioned Aldo Rossi (1931–97) to collaborate with him on one of the buildings.

Both Aymonino and Rossi taught at the Istituto Universitario di Architettura di Venezia and were interested in the theory of urbanism and the development of the modern city. Aymonino and Rossi set about creating a new piece of the city that would function to serve an entire community, in what would become the largest post-war residential quarter in Italy. It was funded by the Monte Amiata Mining company who owned the land, but with a programme drawn up in partnership with the Milan municipality.

The Monte Amiata housing, as it came to be called, was designed between 1967 and 1969 to house 2,400 inhabitants across 444 dwellings. The scheme comprises five buildings: two eight-storey blocks, a long three-storey block and a much shorter three-storey block, all connected by a fifth structure. Four of the buildings were designed by Aymonino and one by Rossi, with huge contrasts between them. Aymonino's warm russet-toned buildings with complex stepped sections, out of which huge cylinders of lifts protrude at regular intervals, drew directly from Trajan's Market in Rome. Primary colours are used sparingly but effectively – raised walkways and piloti are painted canary yellow; blues, reds and yellows adorn the walls of the double-height corridors and all the window frames are a warm red. By contrast, Rossi's building is a 185-metre long, 12-metre deep building in minimalist white, raised above the ground floor colonnade. The facade is perforated by rhythmic square windows in a continuous sequence.

There are a whole range of housing typologies, from courtyard dwellings to duplexes. The buildings are linked by a series of footbridges and public spaces including an impressive open-air theatre resembling a Roman amphitheatre and two piazzas. Plans for social services including a school, nursery and shops along Rossi's colonnade were never realised.

The project was started during the country's 'boom years', but this simultaneously widened the gap between the rich and poor. By the time Monte Amiata was completed in 1973, the country was in recession, and by 1974 the apartments had been taken over by squatters of the Left Proletarian. They criticised the complex for not being low-cost housing – they perceived the unusual architecture and the design, such as the wide corridors and colour scheme, as emblematic housing for the rich. After a few months the squatters were evicted by the police and the finished buildings were acquired by the municipality of Milan, with the apartments reserved for its employees. And so a scheme originally intended to house immigrants flooding into the city of Milan, was now aimed at the growing middle classes. For this reason, politically speaking, the housing complex became one of the most discussed and received much press attention. It has been criticised for the lack of social provisions and for its disconnect from the surrounding suburban spaces. The design of the dwellings also came under scrutiny, with criticisms such as the bathrooms being too far from the bedrooms, kitchens too far from dining rooms and the small units having too few windows. However, many of the first inhabitants still live there today, so its success perhaps speaks for itself.

Serena Cazzulani

Serena, a teacher, and her twelve year-old son live in a two-bedroom duplex in one of the blocks designed by Carlo Aymonino.

Describe the layout of your apartment

It has an open plan living and dining room, a small kitchen, a double bedroom and a bathroom on one floor and upstairs there is another bedroom. Originally the living space would have been double height – similar to the apartments in Le Corbusier's Unité d'habitation, but the previous owners filled it in to gain extra floor space. There are also two balconies.

How long have you lived in Monte Amiata?

I've lived here all my life. My parents bought an apartment here when the estate was first built in 1976, and they still live here today, although in a different apartment. When I wanted to get my own place, I decided to look for something here too. It's quite common that the children of the original residents have stayed and bought their own apartments and had their own families. I've lived in a number of different apartments in the complex, but I've been in this one since 2000.

What attracted your parents to living here?

They liked the size and style of the apartment as well as the overall architecture of the place. At that time, it was quite isolated – there wasn't a metro, for example. They used to live in the centre of Milan and they were drawn to the utopian living the architects envisioned, a 'village within a city'. The architects wanted to encourage communal living – it was the mid-70s and a different time to now. When I was young many of the families and children would be outside together a lot. The children would be out until late playing together. I think the architecture really promotes a sense of community.

Are there many young families living here today?

Yes, there's a new generation of families living here. The area I think is fantastic – with its parks, and lots of open spaces, it's very good for families. Also the cost of the apartments, compared to other properties in Milan, makes it very attractive.

And is there still a sense of community amongst the newer residents?

To an extent there is, but less so. We are trying to promote the social aspect, for example recently we have set up a residents' library, a residents' cinema – where every week we show a film, and a book club. There's a lot of open communal spaces that aren't used very often, such as the open-air theatre, so we are trying to encourage people to use them more. Recently we had a photography exhibition in the 'red corridor'.

The communal areas look very well maintained, who looks after them?

We have an external private management company. Although the apartments in themselves are well priced, the service charges are expensive. We have cleaners, gardeners, maintenance people and two porters who run the car parks all day and that costs a lot. It's all very well managed though – if something breaks down, there is somebody here straight away to fix it.

Has it changed much since you were young?

Not really. A lot of the original residents are still here. The place still feels like a village. And the porters, who are very friendly, have been here a long time.

What is the general perception of the architecture?

Not everybody likes it. A lot of the apartments are deck access which some people associate with social housing. My friends like it – I think they do anyway, if they don't they haven't told me! But I love it, and my son does too. In fact, it has inspired him to want to become an architect.

What are the facilities like?

There used to be several shops here, a baker, bar, dry cleaners, but they have closed down as people are using out-of-town supermarkets. The idea was that there would also be a school on the grounds, but that didn't happen, unfortunately.

What's the general area like?

It's very quiet and relaxed, with lots of green spaces but well connected to the centre. It's a good quality of life.

Above
The living room with door to the private balcony

Above
Looking towards the dining area

Above left
Stairs leading up to the mezzanine

Above right
The second bedroom; the floor has been extended
into what was originally a double-height space

Above left
The kitchen

Above right
The main bedroom

Walden 7

Barcelona Spain

Architects Ricardo Bofill Taller de Arquitectura

Located in Sant Just Desvern, a western suburb of Barcelona, Walden 7 was conceived in the 1970s as a utopian vision of mass housing, its name inspired by the 1948 science-fiction novel *Walden Two* by B.F. Skinner which depicts a utopian community. The architects behind the scheme are Ricardo Bofill (b. 1939) and his practice Taller de Arquitectura. Bofill began his practice in 1963 as a multi-disciplinary group which included a writer, a painter, a sculptor, a philosopher, an engineer and a mathematician.

In the early 1970s Spain was in the twilight of the dictatorship of the Franco regime, but times were changing, and old ideas and attitudes had begun to be challenged. Completed in 1975, the 400 or so apartments at Walden 7 were priced considerably lower than the norm at the time, although it was not social housing per se. The Taller de Arquitectura put community at the centre of Walden 7 in an ambitious and radical way. They saw the building's potential tenants as collaborators in the social experiment. 'Waldenites' were interviewed and selected by Bofill's team, with one of the main requirements being that the residents should be non-conformists, which led to the building being likened to a commune. This is where the like-minded gauche divine of Barcelona would gather, and there are countless stories of decadent parties held on the rooftop.

The building — built on a former cement factory — is composed of eighteen 16-storey towers. The towers are displaced from their base, forming a curve which then comes into contact with the neighbouring towers. The result creates a labyrinth of walkways and bridges around seven courtyards. A large proportion of the building is given to communal spaces, including two swimming pools and a solarium on the roof terrace. The building was originally clad in terracotta clay tiles, influenced by a trip the architects made to the Algerian desert. Internally, the walls are clad in contrasting turquoise and yellow ceramic tiles. The apartments are made of 30-metre square modules — creating modularity by allowing flexibility and reconfiguration of the units. Dwellings range from a single-module studio to a large four-module duplex apartment.

Originally the scheme was intended to be much larger, but due to funding issues only one building was ever completed, and even then it was subject to severe delays. Once the building was finished, technical problems in its construction began to appear. The red tiles that clad the facade began to fall off and residents complained about the lack of light from the small windows. The building suffered years of neglect, but in the 1990s the government finally stepped in and it was restored (at a huge cost) with the majority of the exterior painted rather than re-tiled.

Just next door to Walden 7 is Bofill's La Fabrica, his home and office, and perhaps his most striking building. The converted cement factory, where eight silos remained, was converted to the firm's architecture studio, a library, a projection room and a huge space known as the Cathedral used for exhibitions, concerts and a whole range of cultural functions. The building is surrounded by gardens of eucalyptus, palms, olive trees and cypresses. Despite the close proximity of his studio to Walden 7, Bofill distanced himself somewhat from the project, preferring to look forwards rather than backwards. His practice went on to design a number of large social housing schemes including the Espaces d'Abraxas in Noisy-le-Grand, France. Later projects adopted a more neoclassical style as seen in the Antigone development in Montpellier, France.

Helena Ardevol and Younes Karroum

Helena, a native of Barcelona, and her husband Younes, originally from Haiti, both work in the humanitarian sector. They live in a duplex on the fourteenth floor, and are expecting their first child.

How long have you lived in Walden?
[H] My father moved here in the 1970s when it was first built so I grew up here. I moved away when I was twenty-one but have recently moved back here with my husband as we are expecting our first baby.

What was it like growing up here as a child?
[H] It was amazing. I had the best childhood here. It was a like living in a commune. I think people were more open twenty years ago than they are today, so everyone's doors would be open and you would go in and out of your neighbours' homes. I had lots of friends here and the whole building was a playground for us.

Why did your father decide to move here?
[H] Actually that's a funny story. My father and his friend, a writer, won a million pesetas on the lottery and decided to buy an apartment together. The building hadn't even been built yet, but the apartments were being sold at a cheaper rate to attract younger people so they decided to buy here. Eventually my father's friend moved to the US to live with his girlfriend, so my father bought his share of the apartment, my mother moved here and then they had me and my brother.

What kind of people were living here when your father first moved in?
[H] The first wave of people were artists, architects — Bohemians, I suppose. Because of the lower price of the apartments it attracted a certain type of person — those who were rejected from the mainstream. It was still the time of the Franco regime, and the people who lived here had a shared vision of what they wanted for the future. The way my parents describe it, it was quite wild in the early days. As we came out of the Franco regime people expressed their freedom, and it was like an explosion. There were parties, people smoking marijuana — it was like Barcelona's version of Woodstock! That was before I was born, so I don't remember it, but there was also a

dark side to Walden. Some people got too carried away in the hedonism with some losing their lives to drugs, and there are also dark stories of suicide.

Does your family still live here?
[H] Yes, actually this apartment is the apartment I grew up in. We had some friends who lived next door, and when they moved away we bought their apartment so we could extend. The apartments work in modules of 30 square metres and the idea is that you join flats together as your family grows. We were living here with my grandmother too, so we needed more space. Now we have divided the apartments again, and my mother and father live next door.

When you were a child, how was Walden perceived by your friends who weren't living here?
[H] My friends were fascinated by it, but their parents thought it was horrible and couldn't believe we lived here. This is a working-class area and the building was very radical, especially at that time. Coming out of a dictatorship, it was a very closed society and people were not open minded enough to embrace this new way of living. My father is an architect and my mother is a nurse — they were not bourgeoise as they came from a small village in Catalonia, but they had access to education and were more open to explore new ways of living. That's what I love about it. It's not just a building, it's a concept for how to live your life.

How does the building affect the way you live?
[H] You have privacy in your own apartments, but you are very close to your neighbours so there is a strong sense of sharing and living together. When I was little I could see whether my friends were in or not if their lights were on, so I would just shout out to them from the balcony instead of going to their apartment. When I think back to my childhood, I think that's the kind of life I want my baby to have.

Are there many young families like yours here?
[H] Not really, most of my friends have moved away. The building is not an easy building to live in by modern standards. For example, there's no gas so we have to

have electric heaters. It's very cold in the winter and the electricity is expensive. The service charges we have to pay are also high and you don't get much in return. We pay about 250 euros a month, which is a lot compared to salaries here. It covers the cost of all the cleaning of the walkways, the lift maintenance etc. We also have to have somebody on site here every day doing repairs – there is always something that is breaking down. People who are into the architecture might be interested in living here, this is an expensive suburb – so for some people it's an attractive option – but generally the apartments aren't in demand, many of them are empty.

Why do you think there are so many things that need repairing?
[H] My father says the project was too ambitious. When I was younger and the building wasn't very old I remember things already going wrong – like the tiles falling off the facade. That was a major crisis, and at the time they were considering demolishing the whole building. My father was very involved in saving it.

What are the worst things about living here?
[H] I think the biggest problem is the light. We are at the top on the fourteenth floor, so it's great, but lower down, especially in the apartments that are in the middle of the building, it's very dark. My parents had friends who lived on the second floor; the woman was a housewife so she was at home a lot, and their apartment was so dark she became depressed and eventually they had to move out.

Is the building listed?
[H] It is now. When we decided to move back here, we wanted to do a few things to the apartment such as putting in some more windows, but we are not allowed. They are quite strict about it.

What was it about Walden that made you want to move back here?
[H] Part of the reason is practical – financially it makes more sense for us to live here, and having my parents here when I have the baby will be great. In the main, though, it's not rational – I have a romantic attachment to the building.

And what does your husband think of it?
[H] The first time he came here he was really impressed.
[Y] The first time I saw it I thought it looked like a huge termite mound! The shape, the colour … I thought it was one of the most incredible buildings I had ever seen. There's a strong link between the building and the living experience – it's full of crazy people!

What kind of people live here now?
[Y] Every kind of person you can imagine. You could make a movie about the people who live here – musicians, teachers, drug dealers. It's full of personalities. The space is designed in such a way that you get to see and know them, which is very different from where my family lived. They were Moroccan immigrants who moved to France, and social housing there is completely impersonal. The only interaction you have with your neighbours is complaining about the noise. You don't see or know anyone, you just go into your own place and that's it. This place is full of mystique. It's asymmetrical and there are things about the building that you cannot understand, but it feels human – even though it looks like it's landed from a different planet!
[H] I think it has lost some of the collective lifestyle it once had. We used to have big gatherings on the roof during holidays, but people are less involved in those kinds of things now. When I was little we would go up to the swimming pools on the roof on our own; now you have to be at least fourteen and are only allowed to bring two people with you. For me, this kind of thing makes it ugly, it's against the ethos of the building.

Are there fewer creative people living here now?
[H] I think so, or the creative people are older and don't have the energy they once had. There used to be a group of drag queens living on the second floor and I remember thinking as a child how cool that was. Every floor had a different personality and we have lost a bit of that. But I still love it. A friend of mine moved here a couple of years ago – in the summer he might come over at 11 p.m. for a drink, or my mum and dad pop round and we sit and have dinner outside in the walkway. It's a really lovely lifestyle which I wouldn't want to lose.

Page 177
Stairs from the living room

Above
The original kitchen

Above
The upstairs landing

Above
Upstairs landing with doors to the bedroom

Above left
The bedroom

Above right
View of the upstairs landing
from the bedroom

181

Medina

Eindhoven
The Netherlands

Architect
Neave Brown

When Dutch architect and urban planner Joe Coenen (b. 1949) was Chief Government Architect of the Netherlands between 2000 and 2004, he invited architect Neave Brown (1929–2018) to design new housing in the Small Haven area of Eindhoven. Brown, originally from the US, had worked extensively in the UK designing social housing in the 1960s and 70s for the London Borough of Camden. In a period referred to as 'Cook's Camden' (named after Camden Council's borough architect Sydney Cook), a number of innovative housing projects by Brown and others – including Benson and Forsyth, Peter Tábori and Bill Forrest – were built. They rejected the high-rise developments that had come to dominate the London landscape and sought to return to the vernacular of the city – the street. Brown was a key figure with his project at Alexandra Road in Swiss Cottage, which is widely regarded as a seminal piece of work.

The basic premise of the Alexandra Road scheme is two continuous blocks that run east to west with a central paved walkway running through the middle. The blocks are stepped – allowing for each dwelling to have its own large terrace open to the sky above and its own front door. The project received wide international attention.

The brief for the Eindhoven project was for mixed-use buildings on a site between the ring road (with new commercial buildings beyond it) and an eighteenth-century walkway with old buildings along it. Joe Coenen came up with the idea of a neighbourhood like a 'medina', with stacked houses, shops and small businesses. Having visited the Alexandra Road scheme some years previously and met Brown, a friendship formed, and together with the executive architect (Van Aken Architectuur) and the developer (Hurks Bouw & Vastgoed) they commenced a project of similar ambition for a scheme of live/work apartments.

With his ingenuity in planning and experience with the Alexandra Road scheme, Brown skilfully resolved the dilemma of how to seamlessly link the old city with the new. He created a tall seven-storey barrier block facing the ring road, which steps down, with a series of planted terraces, to three storeys. A new walkway was created at the foot of the building to match the scale of the eighteenth-century walkway, and placed a row of four- and three-storey buildings along it. Commercial units and artists' workshops are positioned on the ground floor along the new pedestrian street, with living accommodation above.

Car parking is placed over two levels in the basement. In total there are seventy-three apartments, 2,000 square metres of commercial space and 250 parking spaces. In the main stepped block the apartments on the first to fourth floors are over two storeys, each with a large, south-facing roof terrace. The apartments on the fifth and sixth floors are single storey with south-facing balconies – and at the top, on the seventh floor, are large penthouses.

The blankets of hanging gardens are a key striking feature of the complex. The planting scheme was designed by Soontiëns Hoveniers as three zones of greenery: public green spaces, collective green spaces and private green spaces. A total of 6,000 plants were planted, with all kinds of variations to ensure a green appearance throughout the year. A key to the success of the complex is the commitment by the residents to maintain the gardens immaculately.

The Medina complex was completed in 2002 and was Neave Brown's last, and possibly best, project. In 2017 he was awarded the prestigious RIBA Royal Gold Medal.

Opposite
The seven-storey facade facing the ring road

Page 184
View of the workshops with accommodation above, along the newly created walkway

Page 185
View from one of the houses looking towards the main building, with tower designed by Joe Coenen in the background

Anton Maréchal

Anton, a former policeman in Amsterdam, is now a consultant in urban security and safety. He lives in a two-bedroom apartment in the main Medina block.

How long have you lived in Medina for?
I've lived here since it was completed in 2002. Building of the complex started in 1999; that's when I saw the plans and decided to buy here. Before that, I lived in a rented property just across the road.

What attracted you to living here?
The developer produced a really wonderful book with all the plans and drawings of the different apartments and the complex. I thought it looked marvellous – I fell in love with it immediately. I've lived everywhere, from small villages to cities, but I love living in the centre of the city and this is incredibly central.

So you were one of the first people to buy here?
Yes, I think I was the first person!

What did you think of it when it was completed?
It was better than I had imagined, and it's got even better since. Initially there wasn't any greenery, and as I was the chairman of the owners' association I was very involved in the decision-making process of what the planting should be.

How does the owners' association work, and why did you become the chairman?
As owners we are financially responsible for the complex as a whole. In particular, the maintenance of all the communal areas, such as the planting, the car parking in the basement, cleaning and the central heating system. We all have to agree on any big expenses – we get together once a month, but we try not to make it too serious and so perhaps have a glass of wine too.

I volunteered to be the chairman as I used to work in real estate after a career with the police in Amsterdam, so I had experience in these kinds of things. I did it for five years but then stepped down. If you stay too long in these roles you become an institution, which isn't good. People would ring me day or night, which wasn't much fun. Then about five years ago, I was asked to be chairman again. I agreed, but it's better now – I'm seen more as a co-owner.

What type of people live here?
It's a mixed community – single people, couples, a few families. There used to be more elderly people at the beginning, but they have either moved or passed away. So now younger people are moving in, which I think is good.

How many of the original owners are still living here?
About 50 per cent I think. There are now also eight or so flats which are rented out.

And do those younger people also take an active role in the association?
Not so much, they are used to having things done for them and don't always take the initiative to do something for the community.

Are there occasions outside of the association where residents get together?
Every year we organise a New Year's get-together in Stratumseind, the street parallel to ours, which is famous for its bars, clubs and restaurants. We sometimes also organise a barbecue.

Describe the layout of your apartment
You enter on the first floor, and there are four rooms: a large storage room (about 16 square metres), the bathroom and toilet, and two bedrooms which lead out to the patio. On the second floor there's a large open plan living room, dining room and the kitchen. Then, outside, there is a little bridge across the patio below, to a very large terrace. I think it's about 100 square metres. When I was living in Amsterdam, I always dreamt of living somewhere with a terrace.

What is it about the architecture that you like?
The front of the building that faces the road is very modern in style, almost industrial, and the other side with the terraces is very different – a green oasis. I think that contrast is fantastic.

Is the planting expensive to maintain?

It's more than a normal building of course, I expected it would be, although some owners didn't. But we all pay for it with a good attitude as it's such an important part of Medina. We all enjoy it immensely.

Is Medina generally well known and liked in Eindhoven?

Now it is because it's been featured in several books. This whole area was designed by Joe Coenen who, at the time, was architectural advisor to the government in the Netherlands, so he's very well known.

Are the apartments sought after? Were they popular straight away?

The apartments were popular, but when they were first sold, ten were bought up by the same company who then sold them off at an increased price, which made them expensive. I don't think that was fair. Now, no one owns more than one apartment here.

Are there any negatives to living here?

For me there are only positives! I have mostly lived in apartments and I think when you live in an apartment you have to understand that it's a different kind of community – especially living in the centre of a city. On Saturdays or special holidays, for example, it can be noisy with the cafes etc. But the insulation of the building is very good so it's not really a problem. I think some people, when they first move here, don't expect it to be so busy, and sometimes as the chairman I have to remind them that if you choose to live so centrally, you have to accept the negatives of the neighbourhood. At the beginning, the cafes and bars didn't really know how to deal with the problem as they weren't used to it being a residential area. It took a couple of years, but we worked with the cafe owners and the council and things are much better now.

I noticed that the complex is gated, was it always like that?

Not at first, but we had some problems with people coming here to drink and take drugs. They would go up on the higher levels where they couldn't be seen by the police. We also had some rough sleepers breaking into the block and sleeping here, so we had to get better security. But it's generally a very safe city.

Do you ever imagine living anywhere else other than here?

I lived in Amsterdam for twenty years and I really love it there. People ask me if I will ever move back and my answer is always, 'Only if I can take my apartment with me'.

Page 189 and above
The living and dining space

Above left
Entrance hallway, with stairs leading
up to the living space

Above right
The main bedroom with small
courtyard beyond

Page 192
Footbridge over the courtyard linking
the living spaces to the terrace